Perfect One-Dish Dinners

Perfect One-Dish Dinners

ALL YOU NEED FOR EASY GET-TOGETHERS

Pam Anderson

PHOTOGRAPHS BY JUDD PILOSSOF

Houghton Mifflin Harcourt
Boston New York 2010

www.hmhbooks.com

Library of Congress Cataloging-in-Publication Data is available.

ISBN 978-0-547-19595-7

Printed in China

Book design by Kris Tobiassen
Food styling by Liz Duffy
Prop styling by Roy Finamore

scp 10 9 8 7 6 5 4 3 2 1

To Flynn and Della

Acknowledgments

Thanks to:

Terrie Brown, my faithful friend in and out of the kitchen. Her keen eye for the good things has decidedly improved mine.

Bob Feinn at Mt. Carmel Wine & Spirits Co., whose wine advice, both for this book and for my table, is invaluable.

Photographer Judd Pilossof, prop stylist Roy Finamore, and food stylist (and Judd's wife) Liz Duffy, the most in-sync photography team I've ever worked with (and gorgeous pictures to boot).

Book designer Kris Tobiassen, whose design perfectly captures this book's simple, carefree feel.

Copy editor Susan Dickinson and typist Jacinta Monniere for their award-deserving eye for detail.

Rux Martin, my astute editor for more than a dozen years.

Sarah Jane Freymann, my cherished agent and friend for even longer.

My friends and colleagues at *USA Weekend,* for letting me be their food voice for nearly a decade.

My friends and colleagues at *Runner's World,* for giving me a regular presence on their pages.

Maggy Keet and Sharon Anderson, my daughters, friends, students, *and* teachers.

And David Anderson, my husband and dinner date for thirty-two years now.

contents

Introduction

The seed for this book was planted a number of years ago, when I was teaching a cooking class in California. A woman raised her hand and confessed, "I can make one dish just fine, but when I have to orchestrate the rest of the meal so it all comes out at just the right time, I get flustered."

Since then I've given a lot of thought to her admission. It *is* stressful to pull off a multi-course, multidish meal. But, with perhaps the exception of the occasional holiday extravaganza, things really don't need to be that complicated. A memorable dinner can be as simple as bringing one beautifully complete dish to the table.

This book features dozens of such dinners that will wow family and guests, calm the cook, and, at the end of the night, impress the dishwasher. Regardless of the season, the amount of time you have to prepare the meal, or the number of guests you've invited, it's easy to find a recipe here that's perfect for the occasion.

I have to confess to a fondness for stews, which is why I include such a wide selection— for any time of the year. Many of the stews in this book, like Jerk Chicken Chili and Braised Lamb Shanks with Tomatoes, Aromatic Vegetables, and White Beans, are classic fall or winter evening fare, but there are plenty of stews for other seasons as well. Coq au Vin Blanc with Spring Vegetables and Salsa Verde Chicken with Herbed Cornmeal Dumplings are ideal for spring, while Spicy Coconut Shrimp Stew with Tomatoes and Cilantro and Carnita-Style Beef with Roasted Peppers and Onions (for a rockin' taco party) are both great for summer.

The possibilities go far beyond stews. Jazz up your next dinner with a decidedly un-American casserole. Doable, Delicious Paella is one of my favorites, as is One-Pot Penne with Turkey-Feta Meatballs—the pasta cooks right in the sauce. Or make lasagna and take your choice of three flavors, all beginning with the same basic step, or choose from three types of enchiladas (Spicy Chicken, Beef and Bean, or Creamy Seafood).

For the holidays, if you dread keeping roast turkey, stuffing, and mashed potatoes hot during the soup course, you might want to relax and join in the festivities by serving one dish such as Festive Roast Chicken or Blue Cheese–Stuffed Beef Tenderloin with Port Sauce and Mushroom-Spinach Barley.

When it's warm outside, the grill becomes the source of some of my most convivial meals. I set out a platter of the grilled version of a classic niçoise salad, enlivened with lemony vinaigrette, or an Antipasto Platter with sausage, shrimp, eggplant, peppers, and tomatoes drizzled with a feta vinaigrette.

You can make one of the spectacular one-dishes in the book and be done, but you'll also find splendidly simple appetizers and desserts that are specially designed for each meal. Before Chicken Potpie with Green Apples and Cheddar Biscuits, you might want to put out a bowl of smoked almonds, but spend just a few minutes more in the kitchen, and you can serve Perfect Spinach-Artichoke Dip. And for when you have even less time, I've given you almost instant alternatives for each meal, which rely on store-bought foods but taste spectacularly homemade. For example, you can end the meal with a buttery Giant Linzer Cookie filled with raspberry jam—or make it with store-bought refrigerated dough, if you're running short on time. You can follow the menus just as is or mix and match them for hundreds of different dinner options.

Whether it's a Super Bowl bash, a surprise birthday, a book club supper, a gourmet gathering, a housewarming party (and, for me, a constant stream of events at the church rectory), or just a Saturday afternoon when you feel like making something special for the family, *Perfect One-Dish Dinners* offers just the right recipes.

Leftovers? No problem—put them to good use for quick weeknight dinners (it's what I call money in the bank). With every dish, you'll find storage and reheating instructions.

So why stress out planning and overseeing a complicated dinner?

Perfect One-Dish Dinners offers a wonderfully freeing alternative. You get to host your dinner—and enjoy it too.

Perfect One-Dish Dinners

Stews for All Seasons

Frogmore Stew

For a big summer party, it doesn't get much simpler than a one-pot Tidewater seafood and sausage boil. The whole process—from making the quick spicy broth to adding sausages and potatoes, followed shortly by corn and, finally, shrimp—takes only 40 minutes.

APPETIZER BLT Rolls
Instant Alternative: Summer Tomato Sandwiches

DESSERT Peach Cobbler
Instant Alternative: Sugared Peaches with Caramelized Pecan Ice Cream

Frogmore Stew

SERVES 8

Arrange this stew on a large platter (or in individual soup plates), garnish with lemon wedges, and give each person a small dish of melted butter for dipping the shrimp and potatoes and spreading on the corn.

The broth can be made several hours ahead, but the stew is simple enough to make, start to finish, right before serving. Warmed on the stovetop or in the microwave, this stew makes a great second meal.

2 **medium onions, quartered from stem to root**

4 **large garlic cloves, smashed**

½ **cup seafood seasoning, such as Old Bay**

   Salt

1 **lemon, halved, plus 2 more cut into wedges**

2 **pounds small red potatoes**

2 **pounds kielbasa, cut into 16 pieces**

8 **ears corn, husked and halved crosswise**

2 **pounds (21–25 count) unpeeled shrimp, preferably wild**

2 **sticks (16 tablespoons) butter, melted**

Bring 3 quarts water, onions, garlic, seafood seasoning, salt to taste, and halved lemon (squeeze its juice into the water before tossing in the juiced rinds) to a boil over medium-high heat in a large heavy roasting pan set over two burners.

Add potatoes and sausage and return to a boil. Cover with foil (or partially cover if using a pot), reduce heat, and simmer until potatoes are just tender, about 20 minutes. Add corn, increase heat to medium-high, and cook, covered, until tender, about 5 minutes longer. Top stew with shrimp; cover and steam for 3 minutes. Turn off heat; gently stir shrimp into hot broth, and let stand, covered, until they are just cooked, about 2 minutes longer. Serve with melted butter and lemon wedges.

DRINK   A chilled light red, such as a Sangiovese or dry rosé

APPETIZER BLT Rolls

MAKES 2 DOZEN

The better the tomato, the better the BLT, so try to find good vine-ripened ones. If you don't want to fry bacon, the store-bought cooked variety is perfectly fine tucked inside these little buns. Although the sandwiches can be assembled quickly, the juicy tomatoes dampen the bread, so make them within a half hour or so of serving.

Salt and freshly ground black pepper

12 **small vine-ripe tomatoes, rounded ends removed, tomatoes cut into 4 slices**

½ **cup mayonnaise**

1 **package (24) small party rolls, halved crosswise**

4 **cups prewashed mixed baby greens**

12 **slices bacon, cooked and quartered crosswise (see headnote)**

Salt and pepper tomato slices. Assemble sandwiches: Spread 1 teaspoon mayonnaise on cut side of each roll top. Place a few salad greens and 2 pieces of bacon on each roll bottom. Add 2 tomato slices to each roll bottom. Cap with top and serve.

INSTANT ALTERNATIVE: Omit the bacon and salad greens from BLT Rolls for simple, straightforward Summer Tomato Sandwiches.

DESSERT Peach Cobbler

SERVES 8 TO 10

This hybrid part cake, part cobbler dessert doesn't get much simpler. You can make it earlier in the day and reheat it in a 300-degree oven for 10 minutes. But for the ultimate experience, bake it while you eat dinner and serve it warm, fresh from the oven.

1   stick (8 tablespoons) unsalted butter

1½ cups bleached all-purpose flour

1½ cups plus 2 tablespoons sugar, divided

2   teaspoons baking powder

½   teaspoon salt

1½ cups whole milk

1   teaspoon almond extract, divided

2   pounds peaches, peeled, pitted, and sliced (about 4 cups)

1   quart premium vanilla ice cream (optional)

Adjust oven rack to lower-middle position and heat oven to 350 degrees. Put butter in a 13-by-9-inch baking pan; set in oven to melt.

Meanwhile, whisk flour, 1½ cups sugar, baking powder, and salt in small bowl. Whisk in milk and ½ teaspoon almond extract until smooth. Toss peaches with remaining 2 tablespoons sugar and remaining ½ teaspoon almond extract. When butter has melted, remove pan from oven. Pour batter into pan and arrange fruit over batter. Bake until batter turns golden brown, 45 to 50 minutes. Cool slightly and serve with ice cream, if desired.

INSTANT ALTERNATIVE: If there isn't time to bake, serve Sugared Peaches with Caramelized Pecan Ice Cream with cookies of your choice, if you like. For 8 people, toss 2 pounds peeled, pitted, and sliced peaches (about 4 cups) with ½ cup sugar and ½ teaspoon almond extract; let stand for 30 minutes. Fold a scant cup glazed pecans (from a 5-ounce package, generally sold in supermarkets with other nuts) into 1 quart softened (15 to 30 seconds on high power in microwave) premium vanilla ice cream.

Just before serving, spoon peaches into eight goblets. Top each with a portion of ice cream. Garnish with remaining glazed pecans.

Spicy Coconut Shrimp Stew

WITH TOMATOES AND CILANTRO ON STICKY RICE

Thai in spirit, this light, fresh shrimp stew has broad appeal. The mild yet intriguing flavors will please nearly all palates— even picky ones.

APPETIZER Tuna Salad with Sushi Flavors on Sesame Rice Crackers
*Instant Alternative: Store-Bought Sushi **or** Pot Stickers with Spicy Soy Dipping Sauce*

SALAD Seaweed Salad (available in seafood stores or large supermarkets; optional)

DESSERT Mixed Sorbets on Sweet Ginger Fried Wontons
Instant Alternative: Lava Lamps

Spicy Coconut Shrimp Stew
with Tomatoes and Cilantro on Sticky Rice

SERVES 6 TO 8

These fragrant, flavorful shrimp are ideal for quick gatherings: As long as the shrimp are peeled, dinner can be pulled off in under a half hour. Up to the point of adding the shrimp, you can make this dish a couple of hours ahead (or even the night before, if you refrigerate it). About 10 minutes before serving, simply add the shrimp and heat.

The shrimp beg for a mound of plain sticky rice. Once rinsed, the rice cooks for 15 minutes and rests for another 15 minutes. If left covered, however, it will stay warm for up to 45 minutes, so start your rice, if you like, up to an hour before serving.

As with most leftover stews, this one makes a terrific quick meal later in the week. When reheating it, make sure you don't overcook the shrimp.

3 **pounds (21–25 count) peeled and deveined shrimp, preferably wild**

   Salt

2 **tablespoons vegetable or canola oil**

1 **large red bell pepper, sliced into very thin 1½-inch-long strips**

4 **scallions, thinly sliced (white and green parts kept separate)**

½ **cup chopped fresh cilantro, divided**

4 **large garlic cloves, minced**

½ **teaspoon crushed red pepper flakes**

1 **can (14.5 ounces) petite diced tomatoes, drained**

1 **can (13.5 or 14 ounces) light coconut milk**

2 **tablespoons fresh lime juice**

   Sticky Rice (recipe follows)

Lightly season shrimp with salt; set aside. Heat oil in a 5- to 6-quart Dutch oven over medium-high heat. Add bell pepper, and cook, stirring, until almost tender, about 4 minutes. Add scallion whites, ¼ cup cilantro, garlic, and pepper flakes. Continue to cook, stirring, until fragrant, 30 to 60 seconds. Add tomatoes and coconut milk and bring to a simmer. Reduce heat to medium and simmer to blend flavors and thicken sauce slightly, about 5 minutes. Add shrimp, partially cover, and continue to cook, stirring frequently, until just cooked through, about 5 minutes more. Stir in lime juice and adjust seasonings, adding salt, if necessary. Mound rice on each plate, ladle shrimp on top or alongside, garnish with scallion greens and remaining ¼ cup cilantro, and serve.

Sticky Rice

SERVES 8

Measure 4 cups jasmine or basmati rice into a 5- to 6-quart Dutch oven. Add water to cover and stir until water becomes cloudy; drain through a colander. Repeat covering rice with water, rinsing, and draining until water is more or less clear, a few rinses more. Return rice to pan. Add 5½ cups water to pan, cover, and bring to a boil. Reduce heat and simmer for 15 minutes. Remove from heat and let rice stand, covered, for 10 to 15 minutes longer.

DRINK　**An Oregon or Alsatian Pinot Gris**

APPETIZER # Tuna Salad with Sushi Flavors on Sesame Rice Crackers

MAKES 2 DOZEN

If sushi's a little pricey (or if you've got a crowd of people who are not sure how they feel about eating raw fish), here's a great solution. Mix a can of tuna with wasabi and mayonnaise, spoon a little on a rice cracker, and garnish with a slice of pickled ginger. If refrigerated, the tuna salad can be made a day ahead, but you may want to add a bit more wasabi before serving. Because they make a more dramatic presentation, black sesame crackers are preferable—if you can find them.

   2 cans (6 ounces each) tuna packed in water, drained and mashed to a paste
   2 medium scallions, thinly sliced
   ½ cup mayonnaise (light or regular)
 3–4 teaspoons wasabi paste (Japanese horseradish)
  24 sesame rice crackers, preferably black sesame
  24 slices pickled ginger

Mix tuna, scallions, mayonnaise, and wasabi in a small bowl. Place a heaping teaspoonful of tuna on each cracker. Garnish with pickled ginger and serve.

INSTANT ALTERNATIVE: Pick up some sushi. Many grocery stores have sushi chefs who make it to order. Or, for an attractively priced alternative, pick up your favorite frozen pot stickers. Following package instructions, cook and serve with Spicy Soy Dipping Sauce: Whisk 2 tablespoons each soy sauce and rice wine vinegar, 2 teaspoons sugar, 1 teaspoon sesame oil, and ½ teaspoon crushed red pepper flakes.

Mixed Sorbets on Sweet Ginger Fried Wontons

SERVES 8

Colorful scoops of sorbet resting on crisp, sugary wontons are a refreshing way to end such an engaging meal. The wontons can be fried up to 2 days ahead and stored in an airtight container.

    2 cups vegetable or canola oil
    ½ cup sugar
    1 tablespoon ground ginger
    16 wonton wrappers from a 12-ounce refrigerated package
    3 pints sorbet (my favorite picks are coconut, mango, and raspberry)
    ½ cup coarsely chopped toasted pistachios

Heat oil in a medium skillet over medium heat until a small cube of bread sizzles when dropped in the hot oil. While oil heats, mix sugar and ginger in a shallow bowl, and, for easy cleanup, set a wire rack over newspaper.

Working with 4 at a time, drop wonton wrappers into hot oil. Fry, turning once, until crisp and golden brown, 1 to 2 minutes. Set on wire rack. As soon as you are able to handle, place each wonton in sugar mixture and coat generously on both sides. Return to wire rack. Repeat with remaining 12 wontons.

Using a 1-tablespoon spring-action ice cream scoop, form 8 generous sorbet balls from each flavor and place on a rimmed baking sheet. Cover if preparing more than a few hours ahead and return to freezer.

Just before serving, place 2 wonton nests, overlapping them slightly, on each dessert plate. Arrange sorbets over wontons. Sprinkle with pistachios and serve.

INSTANT ALTERNATIVE: Not up for frying? Lava Lamps are a simpler but equally festive dessert. Use a 1-tablespoon spring-action ice cream scoop to form 8 generous sorbet balls from each of 3 different pints (flavor choice is yours, preferably different colors) and place on a rimmed pan. Cover if preparing more than a few hours ahead and freeze until dessert time. To serve, stack the 3 different sorbet balls in each of eight champagne flutes (or other slender glasses). Top each with a splash of not-too-dry sparkling wine, such as Prosecco, or an extra-dry (oddly named, since it's sweeter than brut) champagne—you'll need a bottle for every 8 desserts (and perhaps a second bottle at the table for those whose sparkling wine vanishes before their sorbet).

Salsa Verde Chicken

WITH HERBED CORNMEAL DUMPLINGS

By adding a jolt of freshness—both cilantro and scallions are stirred into the dough—this dish one-ups traditional chicken and dumplings. Without losing all the comfort-food feel of the original, this rendition is sassy and utterly simple.

APPETIZER Pimento Cheese with Green Olives and Flatbread Crackers
Instant Alternative: Boursin Cheese with Flatbread Crackers

SALAD Baby Spinach Salad with Mango, Avocado, and Red Onion

DESSERT Miniature Lemon-Raspberry Cakes
Instant Alternative: Lemon Curd Ice Cream with Fresh Raspberries

Salsa Verde Chicken
with Herbed Cornmeal Dumplings

SERVES 6

This stew can be made 2 days ahead up to the point of making the dumplings. Reheat it before topping and baking. If you want to double the recipe, use a large heavy roasting pan set over two burners.

CHICKEN

- ½ stick (4 tablespoons) butter
- ½ cup all-purpose flour
- 1 can (14.5 ounces) chicken broth
- 1 jar (16 ounces) salsa verde (2 cups)
- 1 can (5 ounces) evaporated milk
- 1 large rotisserie chicken, meat deboned and left in large chunks (about 6 cups)

DUMPLINGS

- 1 cup whole milk
- 3 tablespoons unsalted butter
- 1½ cups bleached all-purpose flour
- ½ cup yellow cornmeal
- 1 tablespoon baking powder
- ¾ teaspoon salt
- ¼ cup thinly sliced scallion greens
- ¼ cup chopped fresh cilantro

Chicken: Heat butter over medium-high heat in a large (11- to 12-inch), deep ovenproof skillet or 5- to 6-quart Dutch oven. Whisk in flour to make a paste. Mix broth, salsa verde, and evaporated milk and whisk in all at once. Whisk, vigorously at first, until mixture simmers and thickens to sauce consistency. Stir in chicken, heat through, and cover to keep warm. Meanwhile, adjust oven rack to lower-middle position and heat oven to 400 degrees.

Dumplings: Heat milk and butter in a small saucepan until steamy.

Mix flour, cornmeal, baking powder, salt, scallions, and cilantro in a medium bowl with a fork. Stir in milk mixture to form a smooth, firm dough. Pinch off Ping-Pong-ball-size pieces of dough with your fingers and drop onto chicken mixture. Return chicken to a simmer over medium-high heat. Cover and transfer pan to oven and bake until dumplings are cooked through, 15 to 20 minutes. Serve.

DRINK **A good aromatic white like Viognier or Argentine Torrontes**

APPETIZER # Pimento Cheese with Green Olives and Flatbread Crackers

MAKES 3 CUPS

Serve flatbread crackers (preferably unflavored) with this cheese spread, allowing your guests to break off the size cracker they want. If you can't find flatbread crackers (look for them in the gourmet section of the supermarket or the cracker aisle), any mild cracker will do.

By using pimento-stuffed green olives, you get both the pimento that typically shows up in the spread as well as briny Spanish green olives that add great color and piquant flavor. Buy the cheaper salad olives, which are partially chopped.

Use the food processor grating blade to grate the cheese, then switch to the steel blade to coarsely chop the olives (be sure to pulse, not process), and you've got an hors d'oeuvre for a crowd in about 5 minutes. The cheese spread can be stored in an airtight container in the refrigerator for up to a week.

> 1 **pound sharp cheddar cheese, grated**
> 1 **cup coarsely chopped pimento-stuffed olives**
> ¾ **cup light mayonnaise**
> ¾ **teaspoon Worcestershire sauce**
> ½ **teaspoon freshly ground black pepper**
> 1 **package (6–8 ounces) flatbread crackers (see headnote)**

Mix all ingredients except crackers in a medium bowl. Just before serving, line a 3-cup bowl with plastic wrap. Spoon cheese spread into bowl; press to mold. Turn onto a serving plate, remove plastic wrap, and serve with crackers.

> **INSTANT ALTERNATIVE:** Pick up a box of Boursin cheese and a package of flatbread crackers, if available, or regular crackers. Remove the cheese from its packaging, set it on a small plate, and top with a single sprig of fresh dill, a small step that gives the cheese an elegant, homemade feel.

SALAD ## Baby Spinach Salad with Mango, Avocado, and Red Onion

SERVES 6

This refreshing salad complements the spicy chicken and dumplings.

Instead of the dressing here, you can toss with a generous ½ cup Orange Vinaigrette (recipe follows) or Balsamic Vinaigrette (page 27).

1	package (7 ounces) prewashed baby spinach (about 10 cups)
1	large mango (or 2 small), peeled, pitted, and cut into medium dice or 8 ounces fresh strawberries, hulled and sliced (1¼ cups)
¼	medium red onion, thinly sliced
1	ripe avocado, pitted, peeled, and diced
4–6	tablespoons extra-virgin olive oil
	Salt and freshly ground black pepper
1–1½	tablespoons balsamic or rice wine vinegar

Place spinach, mango or strawberries, onion, and avocado in a large bowl. Just before serving, toss with 4 tablespoons olive oil and a generous sprinkling of salt and pepper. Taste, adding more oil, salt, or pepper, if necessary. Add 1 tablespoon vinegar and toss to coat, adding more, if necessary, to taste, and serve.

Orange Vinaigrette

MAKES 1½ CUPS

The dressing can be refrigerated in an airtight container for a week or more.

½	cup frozen orange juice concentrate, thawed
½	cup rice wine vinegar
½	cup olive oil

Whisk all ingredients in a medium bowl.

DESSERT Miniature Lemon-Raspberry Cakes

MAKES 4 DOUBLE CAKES, SERVING UP TO 8

Even though these cakes look and taste as if they came from an upscale bakery, they're actually just raspberry jam and toasted almonds sandwiched between two store-bought shortcakes. The cream cheese frosting, flavored with good jarred lemon curd (located with the jams and jellies in the supermarket), can be whipped up in just minutes. The cakes can be assembled a couple of days in advance (bring to room temperature several hours before serving them). Most people will opt for a half cake, giving you enough for up to 8 servings.

- 1 **package (8 ounces) cream cheese, softened**
- ½ **stick (4 tablespoons) unsalted butter, softened**
- ½ **cup jarred lemon curd**
- ⅓ **cup confectioners' sugar**
- 2 **packages (4.5 ounces each) shortcakes (8 cakes)**
- ½ **cup low-sugar raspberry jam**
- ¼ **cup toasted slivered almonds**
- 1 **pint fresh raspberries (optional)**

Beat cream cheese and butter in a medium bowl with an electric mixer until smooth. Beat in lemon curd, then sugar until light and fluffy. Set 1 cake, well side up, on each of four dessert plates. Spoon 2 tablespoons jam into each well; sprinkle with 1 tablespoon almonds. Top with remaining 4 cakes, well side down. Using a table knife or an offset spatula, frost top and sides with cream cheese mixture, swirling frosting attractively. Serve, garnishing with raspberries, if you like.

> **INSTANT ALTERNATIVE:** Serve Lemon Curd Ice Cream, a flavor so good I can't believe it's not in every grocery-store freezer case. For 6 people, soften 1½ pints premium vanilla ice cream (for each pint, microwave for 15 to 30 seconds on high power, checking after 15 seconds). Turn ice cream into a medium bowl. Spoon ½ cup of good store-bought lemon curd by tablespoonfuls into the ice cream. Fold until lemon curd streaks ice cream. Spoon into six goblets, topping each with a few fresh raspberries. (You'll need a pint of raspberries.) Serve.

Chicken Potpie

WITH GREEN APPLES AND CHEDDAR BISCUITS

Different enough to intrigue adventurous eaters, friendly enough to attract children, this chicken potpie works for so many occasions—Sunday lunch or supper, a potluck dinner, a meal for a family that's just moved or had a baby.

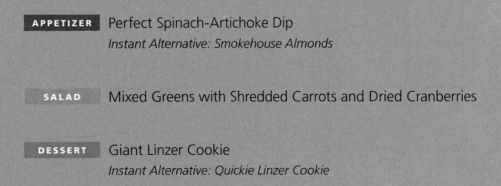

APPETIZER Perfect Spinach-Artichoke Dip
Instant Alternative: Smokehouse Almonds

SALAD Mixed Greens with Shredded Carrots and Dried Cranberries

DESSERT Giant Linzer Cookie
Instant Alternative: Quickie Linzer Cookie

Chicken Potpie
with Green Apples and Cheddar Biscuits

SERVES 8

This recipe makes one big potpie, but to save time or simplify, make two potpies using 9-inch pie plates or 8-inch square baking pans and top with refrigerated store-bought piecrust from a 15-ounce box, following the baking instructions in the recipe. Or freeze the second pie for another occasion, and bake it (still frozen) at 400 degrees until golden and bubbly, about 1 hour.

CHICKEN

2 cups chicken broth

1 can (12 ounces) evaporated milk

¾ stick (6 tablespoons) butter, divided

2 large leeks, dark green leaves trimmed away, washed thoroughly to remove grit, and light green and white parts chopped

2 large Granny Smith apples, quartered, cored, and thinly sliced crosswise

1 large rotisserie chicken, shredded (5–6 cups)

½ cup plus 1 tablespoon all-purpose flour

2 teaspoons dried rubbed sage

¼ cup cream sherry

   Salt and freshly ground black pepper

⅓ cup chopped fresh parsley

BISCUITS

2 cups bleached all-purpose flour

2 teaspoons baking powder

¼ teaspoon baking soda

¾ teaspoon salt

¾ cup grated sharp cheddar cheese

1 stick (8 tablespoons) unsalted butter, frozen solid

1 cup cold buttermilk, plus a few more teaspoons if necessary

Chicken: Adjust oven rack to lower-middle position and heat oven to 400 degrees. Microwave chicken broth and evaporated milk in a microwave-safe bowl until steamy, 3 to 4 minutes.

Heat 2 tablespoons butter in a large (11- to 12-inch) deep skillet over medium-high heat. Add leeks and apples and cook, stirring, until just tender, 7 to 8 minutes. Transfer leeks and apples, along with chicken, to a large bowl; set aside.

Heat remaining ½ stick (4 tablespoons) butter over medium heat in the empty skillet. When foaming subsides, whisk in flour and sage and cook until golden, about 1 minute. Whisk in hot-milk mixture and simmer, stirring, until sauce fully thickens, about 1 minute. Turn off heat, stir in sherry, and season to taste with salt and pepper. Stir sauce, along with parsley, into chicken mixture. Taste and adjust seasonings. Pour mixture into a 13-by-9-inch baking dish or divide between two 8-inch square baking pans or two 9-inch pie plates.

Biscuits: Mix flour, baking powder, baking soda, salt, and cheddar with a fork in a medium bowl. Using a box grater, coarsely grate frozen butter into dry ingredients; mix quickly with fingertips to evenly blend. Mix buttermilk into dry ingredients with a fork until dough just comes together. Pinch dough with fingers into small rough rounds and place over filling. Bake until pastry is golden brown and filling is bubbly, 30 to 35 minutes. Serve.

DRINK **White's the way to go: Pinot Gris, Pinot Blanc, Chenin Blanc, or California Chardonnay**

APPETIZER Perfect Spinach-Artichoke Dip

SERVES 8

There never seems to be enough of this dip at the cocktail parties I attend—people love it. I've sampled a number of spinach-artichoke dips, and this is the best I've ever tasted.

As long as it's in a microwave-safe, ovenproof pan, you can also microwave the dip until it's hot all the way through and broil it on a lower oven rack until the cheese turns golden. Serve with slices of toasted French bread (see page 60), flatbread crackers, or pita chips.

1 **package (8 ounces) light cream cheese (Neufchâtel), softened**

¼ **cup light mayonnaise**

½ **cup finely grated Parmesan cheese**

2 **medium garlic cloves, minced**

½ **teaspoon dried oregano**

¼ **teaspoon salt**

½ **teaspoon freshly ground black pepper**

1 **can (14 ounces) artichoke hearts, drained and coarsely chopped**

1 **package (10 ounces) frozen chopped spinach, thawed and squeezed dry**

¾ **cup grated part-skim or whole-milk mozzarella cheese**

Adjust oven rack to lower-middle position and heat oven to 400 degrees. Coat a 7- to 8-inch decorative baking dish with vegetable-oil cooking spray.

Mix cream cheese, mayonnaise, Parmesan, garlic, oregano, salt, and pepper in a medium bowl until well combined. Stir in artichokes and spinach. Turn into prepared pan, top with mozzarella, and bake until heated through, about 20 minutes. Leaving pan on lower rack, turn oven to broil and continue to cook until cheese is spotty brown, 2 to 3 minutes longer. Let cool for a couple of minutes before serving.

INSTANT ALTERNATIVE: If you're giving this meal to someone else to cook, it may be simpler to pick up a can of smokehouse almonds for the appetizer rather than include another dish that requires baking.

SALAD Mixed Greens with Shredded Carrots and Dried Cranberries

SERVES 8

If the kids don't mind, add a few thinly sliced scallions or ¼ small red onion, thinly sliced. You can toss this salad with about ¾ cup Balsamic Vinaigrette (recipe follows) instead of the dressing here, if you prefer.

10	ounces (about 15 cups) prewashed mixed baby greens
4	large carrots, peeled and grated (about 4 cups)
1	cup dried cranberries
6–8	tablespoons extra-virgin olive oil
	Salt and freshly ground black pepper
1½–2	tablespoons balsamic vinegar

Place greens, carrots, and dried cranberries in a large bowl. Just before serving, toss with 6 tablespoons olive oil and a generous sprinkling of salt and pepper. Taste, adding more oil, salt, or pepper, if necessary. Add 1½ tablespoons vinegar and toss to coat, adding more, if necessary, to taste, and serve.

Balsamic Vinaigrette

MAKES 1 CUP

The dressing can be stored in the refrigerator in an airtight container for a week or more.

1	large garlic clove, minced
⅓	cup balsamic vinegar
2	tablespoons Dijon mustard
¼	teaspoon each salt and freshly ground black pepper
½	cup extra-virgin olive oil

Whisk garlic, vinegar, mustard, salt, and pepper in a 2-cup Pyrex measuring cup. Slowly whisk in oil until you reach the 1-cup mark.

Giant Linzer Cookie

SERVES UP TO 12

I adore everything about this cookie: its distinctive look, its wonderful buttery flavor, and the way it's served—whole, at the table. After that, slice it like a tart or pass it and let people break off what they want. You'll need two 12-inch nonstick pizza pans. The cookies themselves can be made a couple of days ahead and wrapped in foil, but unless you don't care whether the finished cookie softens slightly, it's better to assemble it up to a few hours before serving.

  1 **large egg, plus 1 yolk**
  1 **teaspoon vanilla extract**
  ½ **teaspoon salt**
  2 **sticks (16 tablespoons) unsalted butter, at a cool room temperature**
  1 **cup sugar**
2½ **cups bleached all-purpose flour**
  ½ **cup (half an 18-ounce jar) seedless raspberry jam**
     Confectioners' sugar for dusting

Adjust oven racks to upper- and lower-middle positions and heat oven to 325 degrees.

Mix egg, yolk, vanilla, and salt in a small bowl. Beat butter and sugar in a medium bowl with an electric mixer until smooth and fluffy. Add egg mixture and mix on low speed until blended. Add flour and mix on low speed until dough forms.

Remove ½ cup dough and reserve for another use. (Leftover cookie dough can be rolled ⅛ inch thick, cut into desired shapes, and baked in a preheated 325-degree oven until golden brown, 12 to 14 minutes.) Halve remaining dough, pressing each portion into a 12-inch nonstick pizza pan. Using an approximately 2½-inch round cutter, remove center from 1 cookie. Bake until golden brown, switching and rotating pan positions after 15 minutes, 23 to 25 minutes total. Let cookies stand in pans until firm but still slightly pliable, about 2 minutes. Using an offset spatula, carefully loosen and lift cookies from pans to wire racks to cool to room temperature.

Up to a couple of hours before serving, microwave raspberry jam on high power until partially melted, about 30 seconds. Spread over cookie with no hole, dust cut-out cookie with confectioners' sugar, and place, sugar side up, over raspberry-covered cookie. Serve.

> **INSTANT ALTERNATIVE:** Make a Quickie Linzer Cookie, substituting a 16.5-ounce roll of refrigerated sugar cookie dough. Reduce baking time to 11 to 12 minutes, switching and rotating pan positions after 8 minutes.

Jerk Chicken Chili
Alternative: Vegetarian Jerk Chili

Flavored with warm spices, stewed tomatoes, sweet bell peppers, and pickled jalapeños, jerk chili is perfect for that cold night when you'd much prefer a warmer climate, even for just a few hours.

APPETIZER Mango Guacamole with Tortilla Chips
Instant Alternative: Quick Guacamole with Tortilla Chips

SALAD Arugula with Olives, Corn, Tomatoes, and Scallions

DESSERT Perfect Cupcakes with Pineapple-Ginger Cream Cheese Frosting
Instant Alternative: Gingermen Sandwich Cookies

Jerk Chicken Chili

SERVES 6 TO 8

For a richer, more full-bodied chili, place chicken bones, along with 1 quart broth and 2 cups water, in a pot while preparing the chili ingredients. Bring to a boil, reduce the heat to low, and simmer, partially covered, for 20 to 30 minutes. For a slightly thicker chili, stir in up to 2 tablespoons cornmeal along with the garlic and cilantro.

The chili can be made up to 3 days in advance, and leftovers freeze well. If serving the chili buffet-style, skip the salad, if you like.

  1 **tablespoon olive oil**

  1 **large onion, chopped**

  1 **yellow bell pepper, chopped**

  3 **tablespoons chili powder**

1½ **teaspoons dried thyme**

  1 **teaspoon ground cinnamon**

  ½ **teaspoon ground allspice**

  1 **large rotisserie chicken, meat deboned and shredded (about 6 cups)**

  1 **quart chicken broth**

  1 **can (28 ounces) stewed tomatoes**

  1 **can (16 ounces) black beans, undrained**

  1 **can (16 ounces) small white beans, undrained**

  2 **tablespoons chopped pickled jalapeños**

  3 **large garlic cloves, minced**

  ½ **cup chopped fresh cilantro**

  1 **ounce semisweet chocolate**

Heat oil in a large pot over medium-high heat. Add onion and bell pepper and cook, stirring, until softened, about 5 minutes. Add chili powder, thyme, cinnamon, and allspice. Cook, stirring constantly, until fragrant, about 1 minute. Add chicken and stir to coat with spices. Add broth, tomatoes, beans, and jalapeños, bring to a boil, cover partially, reduce heat, and simmer to blend flavors, about 20 minutes. Stir in garlic, cilantro, and chocolate. Turn off heat, cover, and let stand for 5 to 10 minutes to allow flavors to blend. Serve.

Vegetarian Jerk Chili

Follow recipe for Jerk Chicken Chili, substituting 2 cans (15 to 16 ounces each) drained hominy and 1 can (14.75 ounces) creamed corn for chicken and an equal amount of vegetable broth for chicken broth.

DRINK   **A bold, fruity Zinfandel and for beer drinkers, 6-packs of pale ale**

Mango Guacamole with Tortilla Chips

MAKES 2 GENEROUS CUPS

Once you try this guacamole, you may never go back to the traditional variety again. Mango adds a fresh, sweet dimension to the rich avocado, tart lime, and aromatic cilantro and scallions. If there's time, make the Taste-Like-Fried Tortillas. Not only are they delicious, but your guests can break off the size chip they want.

- 4 small avocados, halved, pitted, and flesh scooped from skin with a spoon
- 1 small mango, peeled, pitted, and cut into small dice
- 2 medium scallions, thinly sliced
- 2 tablespoons chopped fresh cilantro
- 4 teaspoons fresh lime juice
  Salt
  Taste-Like-Fried Tortillas (page 154) or one 14- to 16-ounce bag store-bought tortilla chips

Coarsely mash avocados in a medium bowl with a fork, then stir in mango, scallions, cilantro, lime juice, and salt to taste. Serve with fried tortillas or tortilla chips for dipping.

INSTANT ALTERNATIVE: If you're pressed for time, mash 6 small Hass avocados with a fork until chunky and stir in salt and lime juice to taste. If you can't find ripe avocados, purchase store-bought guacamole and freshen it with a few squirts of lime juice and a sprinkling of salt.

SALAD # Arugula with Olives, Corn, Tomatoes, and Scallions

SERVES 6

Dressed with olive oil and lime juice, this salad is a bright, aromatic partner to the spicy, sweet chili. If serving 8, you'll probably want to increase the salad by half.

7	ounces (about 10 cups) prewashed baby arugula
¾	cup frozen corn, thawed
1	can (2.25 ounces) sliced black olives, drained
3	medium scallions, thinly sliced
1	large tomato, chopped
¼	cup chopped fresh cilantro
4–6	tablespoons extra-virgin olive oil
	Salt and freshly ground black pepper
1–1½	tablespoons fresh lime juice

Place arugula, corn, olives, scallions, tomato, and cilantro in a large bowl. Just before serving, toss with 4 tablespoons olive oil and a generous sprinkling of salt and pepper. Taste, adding more oil, salt, or pepper, if necessary. Add 1 tablespoon lime juice; toss to coat, adding more, if necessary, to taste, and serve.

Perfect Cupcakes with Pineapple-Ginger Cream Cheese Frosting

MAKES 1 DOZEN

Not only does this rich, thick batter make the ultimate yellow cake, but it also makes voluptuous, moist, tender cupcakes. A spring-action ice cream scoop works well for evenly distributing the batter.

Instead of using self-rising flour, you can whisk 1½ teaspoons baking powder and ¼ teaspoon salt into 1½ cups bleached all-purpose flour. Thanks to my son-in-law's grandmother Muriel Mayhew for allowing me to publish her cake recipe.

1½ sticks (12 tablespoons) unsalted butter, softened, plus ½ stick (4 tablespoons) for frosting
1 cup sugar
3 large eggs
1½ cups self-rising flour (see headnote)
1 teaspoon vanilla extract
8 ounces cream cheese, softened
¾ cup confectioners' sugar
1 teaspoon ground ginger
½ cup finely chopped dried pineapple, divided

Adjust oven rack to lower-middle position and heat oven to 400 degrees. Line a 12-cup muffin tin with cupcake liners.

Beat 1½ sticks butter and sugar in a medium bowl with an electric mixer until light and fluffy. Starting and ending with an egg, add eggs and flour alternately, beating until each addition is thoroughly incorporated. Beat in 1 tablespoon warm water and vanilla until just incorporated. Evenly divide batter among cupcake liners.

Bake until golden and a toothpick inserted in center comes out clean, about 15 to 17 minutes. Remove from oven, let cupcakes stand in pan for a couple of minutes, then turn onto a wire rack to cool.

Meanwhile, beat cream cheese with remaining ½ stick butter in a medium bowl with an electric mixer until smooth and fluffy. Beat in confectioners' sugar and ground ginger. Stir in $1/3$ cup chopped pineapple. Frost cupcakes, garnishing with remaining pineapple.

INSTANT ALTERNATIVE: Make Gingermen Sandwich Cookies instead. You'll need two 5-ounce packages Pepperidge Farm Gingerman Homestyle Cookies. Beat 6 ounces softened cream cheese with 3 tablespoons softened unsalted butter until smooth and fluffy. Beat in ½ cup confectioners' sugar and ¼ cup finely chopped crystallized ginger. Smear a scant tablespoon frosting on one side of 16 gingermen cookies. Top with remaining 16 gingermen. (Cookies can be prepared up to 2 hours ahead. After that, the cookies start to soften, but they're perfectly fine that way too.) (Makes 16)

Coq au Vin Blanc

WITH SPRING VEGETABLES

As appealing as the traditional version, this French chicken stew is light and incredibly fast. White wine takes the place of heavier red, while artichokes and new potatoes give the stew a decidedly spring feel (and keep it one-dish). Boneless, skinless chicken thighs instead of bone-in parts, frozen pearl onions rather than chopped fresh, presliced mushrooms instead of whole, prosciutto rather than longer-cooking bacon, dried tarragon instead of fresh, canned chicken broth, canned artichokes—all are legit shortcuts.

And it's a dish that's just as comfortable on china as it is on pottery, so serve it at a nice dinner party or a casual Sunday supper.

APPETIZER Smoked Trout Pâté
Instant Alternative: Smoked Trout with Cream Cheese and Horseradish

SALAD Baby Spinach with Beets, Goat Cheese, and Toasted Walnuts

DESSERT Creamless Chocolate Mousse with Vanilla Ice Cream
*Instant Alternative: Chocolate-Dipped Strawberries **or** Bittersweet Chocolate and a Bowl of Fresh Strawberries*

Coq au Vin Blanc with Spring Vegetables

SERVES 6

The stew can be made 2 to 3 days ahead, but don't add the parsley until you're heating it up.

- 2 pounds (about 8 medium) boneless, skinless chicken thighs
- 2 tablespoons plus 2 teaspoons olive oil, divided
- Salt and freshly ground black pepper
- 1 package (1 pound) frozen pearl onions, not thawed
- 1 package (8 ounces) sliced baby bella mushrooms
- 3 ounces (about 6 thin slices) prosciutto, minced
- 3 large garlic cloves, minced
- ¾ teaspoon dried tarragon
- ¼ cup all-purpose flour
- 1 cup dry white wine
- 2 cups chicken broth
- 1 can (13.75 ounces) whole artichokes, drained and halved
- 2 pounds new potatoes, halved
- ¼ cup chopped fresh parsley

Heat a large (11- to 12-inch) deep skillet over medium-high heat. In a medium bowl, coat chicken with 1 tablespoon oil; sprinkle both sides generously with salt and pepper. Working in 2 batches, add chicken thighs to hot skillet. Cook, turning only once, until well browned, about 6 minutes per batch. Transfer to a bowl and set aside. Add 2 teaspoons oil and onions to skillet and cook, stirring frequently and seasoning with salt and pepper, until golden brown, about 3 minutes. Add to chicken.

Add remaining 1 tablespoon oil and mushrooms to hot skillet and cook, stirring up browned bits and seasoning lightly with salt and pepper, until golden brown, about 3 minutes. Stir in prosciutto, garlic, and tarragon and cook until fragrant, about a minute.

Stir in flour, then wine and broth, along with chicken and onions, artichokes, and potatoes. Bring to a boil, reduce heat to medium-low, and simmer, partially covered, until flavors blend and potatoes are tender, about 15 minutes. Stir in parsley. Cover and let stand for 5 minutes to blend the flavors before serving.

DRINK A white Burgundy—a Pouilly-Fuissé or Saint Veran, for example—or a West Coast Chardonnay

APPETIZER Smoked Trout Pâté

MAKES 2 CUPS

Involving a maximum time commitment of a mere 10 minutes, the pâté is utterly simple and addictive. Be sure not to overpulse the trout. You want to see nice chunks of fish in the cream cheese mixture. Garnish the pâté, if you like, with a sprig of flat-leaf parsley and a sprinkling of freshly ground black pepper. Leftovers keep, covered and refrigerated, for up to a week.

1 **package (8 ounces) light cream cheese (Neufchâtel)**
3 **tablespoons prepared horseradish**
1 **teaspoon Worcestershire sauce**
1 **teaspoon freshly ground black pepper**
1 **package (8 ounces) smoked trout, skin removed**
1 **package (6–8 ounces) flatbread crackers or Melba toasts**

Whir cream cheese, horseradish, Worcestershire sauce, and pepper in a food processor until smooth. Break trout into large chunks into cream cheese mixture and pulse until trout is still chunky but incorporated into cream cheese (about 12 short bursts). Line a 2-cup bowl with plastic wrap. Turn trout mixture into bowl; press to mold. Turn onto a small plate, remove plastic wrap, and serve with flatbread crackers or Melba toasts.

> **INSTANT ALTERNATIVE:** Set 8 ounces of smoked trout on a cutting board along with a 3-ounce block of cream cheese and a small ramekin of horseradish. Set out flatbreads, Melba toasts, or your favorite crackers, and let everyone make his or her own canapés.

SALAD Baby Spinach with Beets, Goat Cheese, and Toasted Walnuts

SERVES 6

This salad reinforces the stew's early-spring quality. Most grocery stores sell cooked beets in the produce department, but it's easy to roast your own. Adjust the oven rack to the middle position and heat the oven to 400 degrees. Wrap each trimmed beet in heavy-duty foil; set them on a small baking pan; and roast until tender, 40 minutes to 1 hour, depending on the size. Cool, peel (the skin rubs right off), and proceed with the recipe. Instead of the dressing here, you can toss the salad with a generous ½ cup Balsamic Vinaigrette (page 27).

7	ounces (about 10 cups) prewashed baby spinach
3	medium cooked beets, chopped (see headnote)
3	ounces (about ⅔ cup) crumbled goat cheese
6	tablespoons chopped toasted walnuts or pecans
4–6	tablespoons extra-virgin olive oil
	Salt and freshly ground black pepper
1–1½	tablespoons balsamic vinegar

Place spinach, beets, goat cheese, and nuts in a large bowl. Just before serving, toss with 4 tablespoons olive oil and a generous sprinkling of salt and pepper. Taste, adding more oil, salt, or pepper, if necessary. Add 1 tablespoon vinegar; toss to coat, adding more, if necessary, to taste, and serve.

DESSERT **Creamless Chocolate Mousse with Vanilla Ice Cream**

SERVES 6

Rather than folding whipped cream into the mousse, which can dull the chocolate flavor, serve it alongside ice cream. With ice cream, you get the softening effects (and save whipping and folding time) without losing the chocolate's intensity and integrity. The mousse can be covered and refrigerated up to a day ahead. Garnish the dessert, if you like, with Pepperidge Farm Chocolate Fudge Pirouette cookies.

- 8 ounces bittersweet chocolate, chopped
- ¼ cup sugar, divided
- 3 large eggs, separated
- 3 tablespoons dark rum
  Pinch salt
- 1 pint premium vanilla ice cream

Melt chocolate and 2 tablespoons sugar in a medium bowl over a pan of simmering water. Remove bowl from heat and whisk in yolks, one at a time, until chocolate is stiff but smooth. Whisk in rum and set aside.

Meanwhile, beat egg whites and salt in a medium bowl with an electric mixer until foamy. Continue to beat, gradually adding remaining 2 tablespoons sugar until stiff peaks form. Stir ½ cup whipped egg whites into chocolate to loosen it. Fold in remaining egg whites until well blended. Cover and refrigerate.

To serve, scoop ⅓ cup mousse and ⅓ cup ice cream into a goblet.

INSTANT ALTERNATIVE: Make Chocolate-Dipped Strawberries. Microwave 3 ounces bittersweet chocolate and 2 teaspoons vegetable oil in a short glass on high power until chocolate just melts, about 1 minute, then whisk to combine. Working with one berry at a time and tilting the glass, dip strawberry to coat completely, shaking lightly to remove excess chocolate. Place on a Silpat baking mat or parchment paper until set, about 30 minutes.

Or simply set out a big bowl of fresh strawberries (2 pints for 6 people), a little confectioners' sugar, and a couple of bars of good bittersweet chocolate (1–2 ounces per person). Let everyone break off a piece.

Shortcut Choucroute

I grew up loving pork and sauerkraut but didn't experience choucroute until early adulthood. With its robust pork broth, hunks of tender pork, and rich earthy sausages, this stew became an instant favorite. But making the traditional dish is an all-day project.

The following recipe can be made with half the effort and in half the time and is every bit as delicious as traditional choucroute. Rather than boiling hocks to make the broth, flavor the stew with instantly enriching prosciutto. Reduce cooking time but retain flavor by using cooked sausages and smoked, cured chops.

APPETIZER Pita Pizzas with Caramelized Onions, Dried Cherries, and Gruyère
Instant Alternative: A Wedge of Gruyère with Focaccia Toasts

DESSERT Avalanche on Mont Blanc

Shortcut Choucroute

SERVES 8

Although it's nicer to serve the steaming pan straight from the oven, you can certainly make the dish a day or two ahead and simply reheat it, like soup, right in the roasting pan. You can also remove the potatoes and freeze the leftovers, adding fresh potatoes to the thawed stew as you're reheating it.

If you can't find smoked pork chops, substitute a good-quality ham, cut into thick slices. Serve with a variety of mustards.

2	tablespoons olive oil
2	large onions, chopped
4	crisp apples, cored and chopped
4	thin slices prosciutto, minced
10	whole cloves
4	bay leaves
2	pounds refrigerated sauerkraut, drained
2	cups dry white wine
1	quart chicken broth
1	pound bratwurst, cut on diagonal into 8 pieces
4	smoked pork chops (about 2 pounds), halved (see headnote)
1	pound kielbasa, cut into 8 pieces
8	red new potatoes, halved

Adjust oven rack to lower-middle position and heat oven to 350 degrees. Heat oil in a large heavy roasting pan set over two burners on medium-high heat. Add onions, apples, and prosciutto and cook until tender and golden brown, about 5 minutes. Add cloves, bay leaves, and sauerkraut and cook, stirring, for a couple of minutes to blend flavors. Add wine, chicken broth, and meats. Bring to a boil, cover with foil, and transfer to oven. Bake to blend flavors, about 45 minutes. Add potatoes, making sure to immerse them in broth as much as possible, and continue to bake until potatoes are tender, about 45 minutes longer. Fish out bay leaves and serve.

DRINK **An Alsatian Riesling or Gewürztraminer or a good German beer**

APPETIZER Pita Pizzas with Caramelized Onions, Dried Cherries, and Gruyère

MAKES 32

The sweet golden onions, kirsch-soaked cherries, and Gruyère are reminiscent of the flavors of Alsace. Pocket-less pitas, which are thicker than ordinary ones, are available in grocery stores.

1 tablespoon olive oil

1 large Spanish onion, halved and thinly sliced

¾ cup dried cherries

2 tablespoons kirsch (cherry brandy)

4 large (7-inch) pocket-less pitas (see headnote)

2 cups grated aged Gruyère cheese (about 5 ounces)

Adjust oven rack to lower-middle position and heat oven to 450 degrees. Heat oil in a large skillet over medium-high heat. Add onion and cook, stirring frequently, until caramel brown, about 10 minutes. Meanwhile, heat cherries and kirsch in a small saucepan over low heat until cherries soften, 4 to 5 minutes.

Scatter a portion of onions and cherries over each pita, then scatter over cheese. Bake until cheese melts and crust is golden brown and crisp, about 10 minutes. Cut each pita into 8 triangles and serve immediately.

> **INSTANT ALTERNATIVE:** Serve ripe pears and a nice French or Swiss cow's milk cheese, such as Gruyère, Beaufort, or Comté, with toasted focaccia or baguette slices (see page 60), flatbread crackers, or your favorite unseasoned crackers.

DESSERT Avalanche on Mont Blanc

SERVES 8

You may think of chestnuts as a savory food, but like any nut, they are excellent paired with chocolate. This dessert is my version of the classic French dessert Mont Blanc, which is sweetened chestnut puree topped with sweetened whipped cream. Here, the dish is inverted: Brandy-flavored snowy whipped cream cascades over chocolate-chip ice cream (the mountain), with chocolate shavings and chestnut "boulders" as part of the avalanche. The whipped cream can be refrigerated and the ice cream mounds frozen for several hours before serving, simplifying assembly. And if you can't find chestnuts, you can make your boulders out of chocolate-covered almonds.

1 **cup heavy cream**

4 **teaspoons brandy**

1 **quart premium chocolate–chocolate chip ice cream**

16 **vacuum-packed chestnuts, coarsely crumbled (see headnote)**

1 **ounce bittersweet chocolate, coarsely grated or shaved with a vegetable peeler**

Whip cream and brandy in a medium bowl with an electric mixer to stiff but billowy peaks. Microwave ice cream on high power to soften slightly, 15 to 30 seconds, checking after 15 seconds. Spoon ice cream into 8 mounds in a 13-by-9-inch pan and return to freezer. Just before serving, place 1 ice cream mound on each of eight dessert plates. Top with ¼ cup whipped cream, letting it cascade down ice cream. Sprinkle chestnuts over desserts so they fall down sides as well. Garnish with chocolate. Serve.

Cassoulet-Style Italian Sausages and White Beans

I adore cassoulet, the French country casserole of duck confit, braised lamb, pork, and beans. In this version, I've pared the dish down to its essence: pork and beans. It's virtually effortless and on the table in under an hour. It's easy enough for a weeknight, special enough for a casual party.

APPETIZER Roasted Almond and Cream Cheese–Stuffed Green Olives
Instant Alternative: Olive Mix and a Bowl of Roasted Almonds

SALAD Mixed Baby Greens with Grapefruit, Celery Root, and Shaved Parmesan

DESSERT Gingersnap-Caramel Pear Parfaits
Instant Alternative: Roasted Pears with Caramel Sauce

Cassoulet-Style Italian Sausages and White Beans

SERVES 8

If there's time, sprinkle buttered bread crumbs over each plated portion for a nice touch. Heat a medium skillet over medium-low heat. Toss 2 cups fresh bread crumbs (made in the food processor from a good European-style loaf) with 2 tablespoons melted butter and a light sprinkling of salt. Add the crumbs to the skillet and cook, stirring frequently, until golden brown, about 15 minutes.

Stored in the refrigerator and warmed on the stovetop or in the microwave, this dish means instant dinner later in the week.

2½	pounds sweet Italian sausage links
3	pints cherry tomatoes
1	medium-large onion, cut into 1½-inch chunks
4	large garlic cloves, sliced
3	tablespoons extra-virgin olive oil
1½	tablespoons balsamic vinegar
2	teaspoons dried thyme
3	bay leaves
	Salt and freshly ground black pepper
3	cans (about 16 ounces each) white beans, undrained

Adjust oven rack to lowest position and heat oven to 425 degrees.

Mix sausages, tomatoes, onion, garlic, olive oil, vinegar, thyme, bay leaves, and a generous sprinkling of salt and pepper in a large heavy roasting pan. Set pan in oven and roast until sausages are brown and tomatoes have reduced to a thick sauce, about 45 minutes. Remove from oven, stir in beans, and continue to roast until casserole has heated through, about 10 minutes longer. Fish out bay leaves and serve.

DRINK An earthy, full-flavored Languedoc or Grenache

APPETIZER Roasted Almond and Cream Cheese–Stuffed Green Olives

MAKES ABOUT 2 DOZEN

The mixture of textures and tastes in these stuffed olives—creamy, nutty, crunchy, and briny—keeps guests coming back for more. Covered and refrigerated, these hors d'oeuvres can be made several hours ahead, but the further ahead you make them, the more the almonds will soften.

1	jar (10 ounces) Spanish Queen (colossal) olives
24	roasted salted almonds
1	block (3 ounces) cream cheese

Remove pimento from each olive and cut a thin sliver off bottom of olive so that it will stand up. Scrape an almond tip over cream cheese to pick up a generous ¼ teaspoon. Stuff almond into olive with cream-cheese tip pointing up. Set on serving tray and repeat with remaining olives.

INSTANT ALTERNATIVE: Set out a bowl of olives and another of roasted salted almonds. Pick a mix of olives. If they are packed in brine, drain them and toss with a little extra-virgin olive oil. Stir in a little finely grated lemon or orange zest and a sprinkling of fresh thyme leaves. Before serving, place nuts in a pan just large enough to hold them in a single layer and warm in a 350-degree oven for 8 to 10 minutes, a small step that intensifies the fragrance and flavor.

SALAD Mixed Baby Greens with Grapefruit, Celery Root, and Shaved Parmesan

SERVES 8

Celery root adds crunch, grapefruit offers a burst of fresh tart flavor, and Parmesan brings a nutty depth to this salad. Don't let the gnarled, knobby look of celery root intimidate you. With a mild celery flavor and a root vegetable texture, it's a great salad ingredient. Simply peel it with a sharp knife and grate on the coarse side of a box grater. If you prefer, instead of the dressing here, toss the salad with about ¾ cup Balsamic Vinaigrette (page 27).

3	medium grapefruits
10	ounces (about 15 cups) prewashed mixed baby greens
1	medium celery root, peeled and grated
¾	cup shaved (with a vegetable peeler) Parmesan cheese
6–8	tablespoons extra-virgin olive oil
	Salt and freshly ground black pepper
1½–2	tablespoons balsamic or rice wine vinegar

With a large knife, cut off tops and bottoms of grapefruits and stand on end. Slicing along sides, cut off rind and white pith using a small sharp knife. Working over a bowl to catch juice, slice between membranes to cut out segments.

Place greens, grapefruit segments, celery root, and Parmesan in a large bowl. Just before serving, toss with 6 tablespoons olive oil and a generous sprinkling of salt and pepper. Taste, adding more oil, salt, or pepper, if necessary. Add 1½ tablespoons vinegar with a little of the reserved grapefruit juice; toss to coat, adding more vinegar or juice, if necessary, to taste, and serve.

Gingersnap-Caramel Pear Parfaits

SERVES 8

For these simple yet impressive seasonal parfaits, the caramel sauce and pears can be made a day ahead and covered and refrigerated separately. They are easy to assemble—a job you can readily delegate. If you like, omit the brandy; the moisture from the cream will soften the cookies.

½   **stick (4 tablespoons) butter**
1   **cup packed dark or light brown sugar**
4   **firm but ripe Bartlett pears, halved and cored**
2   **cups heavy cream**
2   **tablespoons sugar**
6   **tablespoons brandy or cognac, divided**
40   **small gingersnap cookies**

Adjust oven rack to middle position and heat oven to 400 degrees.

Melt butter in a 13-by-9-inch pan in oven until nutty golden. Sprinkle brown sugar over butter, then place pears, cut side down, on sugar. Bake until pears are tender and sauce is thick and caramel-colored, about 40 minutes. Remove pears from sauce and pour sauce into a measuring cup (you should have about 1 cup; if not, boil to reduce or add water to equal 1 cup). Cool pears and sauce to room temperature. Cut each pear half into 8 chunks.

When ready to assemble, whip cream to soft peaks in a medium bowl with an electric mixer, gradually adding sugar. Stir in 2 tablespoons brandy or cognac.

Lightly brush 24 gingersnaps with some of the remaining ¼ cup brandy. Arrange 3 cookies in each of eight goblets. Drizzle each with a little of the caramel sauce and add a dollop of whipped cream and 4 pear pieces. Lightly brush remaining 16 cookies with brandy and repeat layering with 2 cookies in each goblet, caramel sauce, whipped cream, and 3 pear pieces. Repeat again with remaining caramel sauce and whipped cream. Cover and refrigerate for at least 1 and up to 4 hours. When ready to serve, garnish with remaining pear pieces and a final drizzle of sauce.

> **INSTANT ALTERNATIVE:** Roast pears as instructed above, stirring ½ cup heavy cream into caramel sauce once it's in the measuring cup. Place each pear half in a goblet. Drizzle with sauce (a sprinkling of chopped toasted walnuts or hazelnuts is good) and serve.

Pork Stew
WITH SWEET POTATOES AND PRUNES

Sweet potatoes and prunes make fine dish mates for pork. This high-heat stewing technique, coupled with roasting the vegetables alongside, ensures utterly tender meat, rich thick juices, and highly flavored vegetables. If you prefer, you can substitute another root vegetable—new potatoes, turnips, winter squash, parsnips, carrots, or a combination—for the sweet potatoes.

APPETIZER White Bean, Arugula, and Red Pepper Crostini
Instant Alternative: Gnocchi with Parmesan and Sage Butter

SALAD Baby Greens with Fennel, Blue Cheese, and Red Onion

DESSERT Pecan Pie Sundaes
Instant Alternative: Vanilla Ice Cream with Maple Syrup Drizzle and Glazed Pecans

Pork Stew
with Sweet Potatoes and Prunes

SERVES 6 TO 8

The stew, including the roasted sweet potatoes, can be made up to 3 days ahead, stored in the refrigerator, and then reheated. You can easily double the stew using a large heavy roasting pan (see page 66 for instructions).

3   pounds boneless pork shoulder (or boneless country ribs), cut into 1½-inch cubes and patted dry

5   tablespoons vegetable or olive oil, divided

    Salt and freshly ground black pepper

1   large onion, chopped

3   large garlic cloves, minced

2   teaspoons dried thyme

3   tablespoons all-purpose flour

3   cups chicken broth

1   cup full-bodied red wine

4   medium sweet potatoes (2 pounds), peeled and cut into 1½-inch chunks

1½ cups pitted prunes

Adjust oven racks to lowest and middle positions and heat oven to 450 degrees. Heat a heavy-bottomed soup kettle or large Dutch oven over low heat.

Meanwhile, place pork in a medium bowl. Pour 2 tablespoons oil over meat, season with salt and pepper, and toss to coat.

Increase heat to a strong medium-high until wisps of smoke start to rise from the pan. Working in 2 batches to prevent overcrowding, add pork and sear, turning only once, until 2 sides form an impressive brown crust, 6 to 8 minutes per batch. Transfer meat to a plate; set aside.

Add onion to pan, adding 1 tablespoon oil if pan is dry, and cook, stirring, until softened, about 5 minutes. Add garlic and thyme and cook until fragrant, about 1 minute. Whisk in flour, then broth and wine. Return pork to pan. Using two potholders to protect hands, place a sheet of heavy-duty foil over pan, pressing down on foil so that it touches stew. Seal foil around edges. Place lid snugly on pan and let cook until you hear juices bubble. Set pan on middle rack in oven and cook for 1 hour and 15 minutes.

After 45 minutes, toss sweet potatoes with remaining 2 tablespoons oil and a sprinkling of salt and pepper in a 13-by-9-inch pan. Set on bottom rack and roast until sweet potatoes and pork are tender, about 30 minutes longer. Remove sweet potatoes and stew from oven. Remembering that pan and lid are hot, stir sweet potatoes and prunes into stew. Re-cover pan with foil and lid and let meat rest and vegetables marry with stew, about 15 minutes. Set stew over low heat, if necessary, to reheat, and then serve.

DRINK **A hearty Zinfandel or Australian Shiraz**

APPETIZER White Bean, Arugula, and Red Pepper Crostini

MAKES 2 DOZEN

These festive toasts are a flavorful yet inexpensive nibble leading up to the pork stew. The bean mixture can be made ahead, but it's best to stir the arugula into the warm beans just before assembly. If making the toasts more than a few hours ahead, bake them until crisp throughout. Otherwise they tend to stale and toughen.

- **1 baguette, cut into twenty-four ½-inch rounds**
- **1 tablespoon olive oil**
- **2 large garlic cloves, minced**
- **¼ teaspoon crushed red pepper flakes**
- **1 ounce (about 2 thin slices) prosciutto, minced**
- **1 can (16 ounces) small white beans, undrained**
- **1 teaspoon balsamic vinegar**
- **2 cups coarsely chopped arugula**
- **2 jarred roasted red peppers, cut into 48 short, thin strips**

Adjust oven rack to lower-middle position; heat oven to 425 degrees. Place bread rounds on a wire rack; toast until golden brown, 5 to 6 minutes. Remove from oven; set aside.

Meanwhile, heat oil, garlic, pepper flakes, and prosciutto in a medium skillet over medium heat until they sizzle, to bring out flavors. Add beans and cook, stirring frequently and smashing some with a fork, until mixture mounds on a spoon, about 5 minutes. Add vinegar and stir in arugula until it wilts; remove from heat.

Top each toast with a rounded tablespoon of warm bean mixture. Garnish with pepper strips and serve.

> **INSTANT ALTERNATIVE:** Serve Gnocchi with Parmesan and Sage Butter. Bring 1 gallon water and 2 tablespoons salt to a boil in a large pot. Using package times as a guide, boil a 1-pound bag frozen gnocchi, partially covered, until tender. Drain and turn out into a wide bowl or lipped platter. Drizzle with 4 tablespoons butter melted with 2 tablespoons minced fresh sage. Sprinkle with ½ cup finely grated Parmesan cheese and serve on a platter with toothpicks.

SALAD Baby Greens with Fennel, Blue Cheese, and Red Onion

SERVES 8

Crisp fresh fennel, tangy blue cheese, and peppery red onion complement the rich sweet stew. Instead of the dressing here, you can toss the salad with ¾ cup Balsamic Vinaigrette (page 27), if you want.

10	ounces (about 15 cups) prewashed mixed baby greens
1	medium fennel bulb, cored and thinly sliced
½	medium red onion, thinly sliced
4	ounces crumbled blue cheese (about ¾ cup)
6–8	tablespoons extra-virgin olive oil
	Salt and freshly ground black pepper
1½–2	tablespoons balsamic or rice wine vinegar

Place greens, fennel, onion, and cheese in a large bowl. Just before serving, toss with 6 tablespoons olive oil and a generous sprinkling of salt and pepper. Taste, adding more oil, salt, or pepper, if necessary. Add 1½ tablespoons vinegar and toss to coat, adding more, if necessary, to taste, and serve.

DESSERT Pecan Pie Sundaes

SERVES UP TO 12

These sundaes have all the lusciousness of pecan pie—without all the baking time and effort. Since the sauce can be refrigerated for at least a month, the baked pie wedges can be frozen (wrapped in foil and enclosed in a freezer bag) for up to a month, and the glazed pecans are fine in the pantry, you've got dessert in the bank for another time.

  1 **cup plus 2 tablespoons sugar, divided**
  ¾ **stick (6 tablespoons) butter, plus 1 tablespoon butter, melted, divided**
  2 **tablespoons molasses**
  ½ **cup heavy cream**
  1½ **teaspoons ground cinnamon**
  1 **9-inch refrigerated piecrust**
  1½ **quarts premium vanilla ice cream**
  1 **bag (5 ounces) glazed pecans, coarsely chopped**

To make caramel sauce, bring 1 cup sugar and ¼ cup water to a boil over medium heat in a medium heavy-bottomed saucepan, whisking constantly. When mixture starts to boil, turn heat to medium-low and stop whisking. Continue to boil until mixture turns golden brown, 10 to 15 minutes. Remove pan from heat and whisk in 6 tablespoons butter and molasses. When butter has melted, whisk in cream. Cool to room temperature.

Adjust oven rack to lower-middle position and heat oven to 375 degrees. Line a baking sheet with a Silpat baking mat or parchment paper.

Mix remaining 2 tablespoons sugar with cinnamon in a small bowl. Unroll pie dough and place on baking sheet. Brush with remaining 1 tablespoon melted butter and sprinkle with cinnamon sugar. Cut dough into 12 triangles with a pizza wheel or sharp knife and pull triangles out a little to separate. Bake until golden brown, 12 to 14 minutes. Just before serving, scoop ½ cup ice cream into each goblet. Top with 2 tablespoons sauce, a scant 2 tablespoons pecans, and a wedge of pastry. Serve immediately.

> **INSTANT ALTERNATIVE:** Make a simpler pecan pie sundae by scooping premium vanilla ice cream (½ cup per person) into a goblet. Drizzle each serving with 2 tablespoons pure maple syrup, and sprinkle each with 2 tablespoons store-bought glazed pecans. Skip the pastry triangles and serve with a good spice cookie.

Osso Bucco
WITH DIRTY POLENTA

Braised until the veal shanks are fall-off-the-bone tender, osso bucco is traditionally served with saffron-flavored risotto. Unlike risotto, which needs frequent stirring and doesn't hold particularly well, instant polenta cooks in just a couple of minutes, making it possible to cook it in the osso bucco pot once you've transferred the shanks to a platter to rest.

APPETIZER Tomato, Basil, and Mozzarella in Crisp Prosciutto Cups
Instant Alternative: Prosciutto Lollipops

SALAD Steamed Broccoli Vinaigrette with Toasted Pine Nuts

DESSERT Rum-Raisin Cheesecake with Gingersnap Crust
Instant Alternative: Store-Bought Cheesecake with Quick Rum-Raisin Sauce

Osso Bucco with Dirty Polenta

SERVES 6

The shanks are served on a bed of ocher-colored polenta, made rich gold by the spice turmeric. The shanks can be made and refrigerated a few days ahead. Make the polenta just before serving. Instead of the turmeric, you can flavor the polenta with saffron (just add a couple of pinches to the heating water).

6 veal shanks, tied around the circumference with butcher's twine

2 tablespoons olive oil

   Salt and freshly ground black pepper

½ stick (4 tablespoons) butter, divided

1 large carrot, chopped

1 large celery stalk, chopped

1 large onion, chopped

3 large garlic cloves, minced

6 thin slices prosciutto (about 3 ounces), minced

1 tablespoon Italian seasoning

1 can (14.5 ounces) petite diced tomatoes, undrained

1 cup dry white wine

2 cups chicken broth

1½ cups instant polenta

¾ teaspoon ground turmeric

¾ cup finely grated Parmesan cheese

Adjust oven rack to lower-middle position and heat oven to 450 degrees. Heat a large heavy roasting pan set over two burners on low heat. Coat both sides of shanks with oil and season generously with salt and pepper. Increase heat to a strong medium-high until wisps of smoke start to rise from pan. Add shanks and cook, turning only once, until brown on both sides, about 6 minutes total. Transfer to a baking sheet.

Add 2 tablespoons butter to roasting pan and heat. Add carrot, celery, and onion and cook, stirring, until soft and lightly browned, about 3 minutes. Add garlic, prosciutto, and Italian seasoning and cook, stirring, until fragrant, 30 seconds to 1 minute longer. Add tomatoes, wine, and broth, bring to a simmer, return shanks to pan, and turn off heat. Using two potholders to protect hands, place a piece of heavy-duty foil over pan, pressing down on foil so that it touches stew. Seal foil completely around the edges. Repeat with a second sheet of foil so that roasting pan is as airtight as possible. Cook until juices bubble. Set pan in oven and cook for 1 hour and 15 minutes.

Remove pan from oven, transfer veal shanks to a serving platter, cover with foil, and pour sauce into a medium saucepan set over low heat. Add 6 cups water and 1½ teaspoons salt to unwashed roasting pan and bring to a boil. Whisk in polenta and turmeric and continue to whisk until soft but thick, 4 to 5 minutes. Stir in remaining 2 tablespoons butter and cheese. Spoon a portion of polenta onto each of six plates. Top each with a veal shank and a portion of sauce and serve.

DRINK Any medium-bodied Italian red—Valpolicella, Chianti Classico, or Barbaresco from the Piedmont region—or Burgundy or Pinot Noir

APPETIZER # Tomato, Basil, and Mozzarella in Crisp Prosciutto Cups

MAKES 2 DOZEN

Line mini muffin tins with thin prosciutto slices, bake in a moderate oven, and you've got crisp, edible cups. Fill them with the tomato, basil, and mozzarella, or come up with your own filling—fresh melon, pasta salad, egg salad, or marinated seafood, for example. The cups can be made a day ahead, but crisp them up in a 300-degree oven for 5 to 7 minutes before filling.

    12   thin slices prosciutto, preferably prosciutto di Parma, halved crosswise
    12   bocconcini (small mozzarella balls), quartered
    12   grape tomatoes, halved if small, quartered if large
         Generous ¼ teaspoon dried basil
    1½   teaspoons extra-virgin olive oil
         Salt and freshly ground black pepper

Adjust oven rack to lower-middle position and heat oven to 325 degrees. Fit 1 piece of prosciutto into each of 24 mini muffin cups. Bake until they firm up and darken in color, 20 to 25 minutes. Remove from oven, and transfer prosciutto cups to a wire rack to cool.

Meanwhile, mix mozzarella, tomatoes, basil, olive oil, and a light sprinkling of salt and pepper in a small bowl. Fill each prosciutto cup with 2 pieces mozzarella and 1 piece tomato (or 2 pieces if quartered). Serve.

INSTANT ALTERNATIVE: Make Prosciutto Lollipops by mixing 6 tablespoons light mayonnaise and 2 tablespoons Dijon mustard. Spread a teaspoon or so of the Dijon mixture over 18 thin slices prosciutto (preferably prosciutto di Parma). Lift prosciutto off work surface. Stand a 4- to 5-inch breadstick (longer breadsticks can be cut to length) over prosciutto. Twirling breadstick, wrap prosciutto around it to form a "lollipop." Repeat with remaining breadsticks and prosciutto slices to make 18 hors d'oeuvres. Arrange in a short glass and serve.

Steamed Broccoli Vinaigrette with Toasted Pine Nuts

SERVES 6

Especially in the winter, when salad greens are out of season, I love single-vegetable salads like this one, in which broccoli crowns are drizzled with a bright mustardy vinaigrette. The broccoli can be steamed several hours ahead, cooled to room temperature, and covered loosely with plastic wrap. The dressing keeps for days in the fridge. To toast the pine nuts, heat a small skillet over medium-low heat. Add pine nuts and toast, stirring frequently, until golden brown, 5 to 6 minutes.

- 3 **large broccoli crowns, halved**
- **Salt**
- 1 **large shallot, minced**
- 2 **tablespoons fresh lemon juice**
- 2 **tablespoons Dijon mustard**
- 1 **tablespoon rice wine vinegar**
- **Freshly ground black pepper**
- ½ **cup extra-virgin olive oil**
- ¼ **cup pine nuts, toasted (see headnote)**

Place broccoli, ¾ cup water, and a scant ½ teaspoon salt in a large, deep skillet; cover (with foil if there is no lid) and place over high heat. When steam starts to rise from pan, set timer, and steam until broccoli is bright green and crisp-tender, about 5 minutes. Transfer broccoli (do not rinse under cold water) to a paper towel and let stand until ready to serve.

Whisk shallot, lemon juice, mustard, vinegar, and a sprinkling of salt and pepper in a small bowl or 1-cup liquid measuring cup. Slowly whisk in oil, first in droplets, then in a steady stream, to make a thick vinaigrette.

Place a halved broccoli crown on each of six small plates, drizzle with vinaigrette, sprinkle with pine nuts, and serve.

Rum-Raisin Cheesecake with Gingersnap Crust

SERVES 12 TO 16

This cheesecake, which starts from a couldn't-be-easier base of whole ginger cookies, takes very little hands-on time, but you'll need to plan ahead. In fact, the cheesecake is best made up to 3 days in advance so there's time for the flavors to develop. Leftovers freeze well (wrap in plastic and store in a freezer bag for up to 3 months), so put them away for another time when you need a special dessert.

3	tablespoons unsalted butter, melted
2	tablespoons plus 1¼ cups sugar, divided
24	gingersnaps, preferably Nabisco
2	pounds cream cheese (regular or light Neufchâtel), softened
4	large eggs
⅓	cup dark rum
1	cup dark raisins
4	teaspoons all-purpose flour

Adjust oven rack to middle position and heat oven to 375 degrees. Bring 1 quart water to a boil for a water bath.

Mix butter and 2 tablespoons sugar until well mixed. Coat a 9-inch springform pan with vegetable-oil cooking spray. Place a single layer of gingersnaps, flat side down, on pan bottom (there will be spaces between them), and generously brush with butter mixture. Brush flat sides of remaining gingersnaps with remaining butter mixture and place them, rounded side out and slightly tilted toward outer edge, around pan sides. Bake until sugar on cookies bubbles, about 7 minutes. Remove from oven and reduce oven temperature to 325 degrees.

Meanwhile, beat cream cheese in a large bowl with an electric mixer until fluffy. Gradually add remaining 1¼ cups sugar and beat on medium speed until sugar dissolves, about 3 minutes. Add eggs, one at a time, beating until just incorporated and scraping down sides after each addition. Beat in rum. Toss raisins with flour and stir into batter. Cover exterior of springform pan with a double sheet of heavy-duty foil to ensure that no water can seep in; set in roasting pan. Pour batter into springform pan.

Set roasting pan on oven rack and pour in enough hot water to come about halfway up the side of the springform pan. Bake until perimeter of cake is set but center jiggles when pan is tapped, 55 to 60 minutes. Remove pan from oven and let stand in water bath for 30 minutes. Remove springform pan from water bath and set on a wire rack; cool to room temperature. Cover and refrigerate until chilled, at least 4 hours. Slice and serve.

INSTANT ALTERNATIVE: If there's no time to make cheesecake, buy one from the frozen section of your supermarket and serve with Quick Rum-Raisin Sauce, which is equally delicious spooned over ice cream. Warm ½ cup dark rum and ¾ cup dark raisins in a medium saucepan over medium-low heat, then transfer to a small bowl; set aside. Add 1 cup sugar and ¼ cup water to rinsed saucepan. Whisking constantly, bring to a boil over medium-high heat. When mixture starts to boil, turn heat to medium-low and stop whisking. Continue to boil until mixture turns golden brown, 7 to 10 minutes. Remove pan from heat, whisk in 1 cup heavy cream, and stir in raisin mixture. Place over low heat and whisk in 2 tablespoons cornstarch mixed with 2 tablespoons water. Continue to simmer, whisking, until mixture thickens. Cool to room temperature. Sauce can be refrigerated in an airtight container for up to 1 week. (Makes 2 cups)

Rioja Beef

WITH CHICKPEAS, PEPPERS, AND SAFFRON

Meat lovers crave a good stew, and this one, with its Spanish leanings, is both intriguing and appealing. Red and yellow bell peppers, chickpeas, saffron, orange, and paprika bring a fresh twist to a familiar dish.

APPETIZER Sautéed Chorizo Bites with Sweet and Sour Fig Sauce
Instant Alternative: Manchego Cheese with Quince Paste

SALAD Baby Greens with Pimento-Stuffed Olives, Celery, and Toasted Almonds

DESSERT Creamy Flan
Instant Alternative: Dulce de Leche Ice Cream

Rioja Beef
with Chickpeas, Peppers, and Saffron

SERVES 6 TO 8

Colorful peppers brighten this rich stew, while chickpeas provide the starch. It can be made and refrigerated up to 3 days ahead. Simply reheat on the stovetop or in the microwave before serving. As with the other stews in the section, you can easily double the recipe by using a large heavy roasting pan (see page 66 for instructions).

3	pounds boneless beef chuck, cut into 1½- to 2-inch cubes and patted dry
3	tablespoons vegetable or olive oil, divided
	Salt and freshly ground black pepper
1	large yellow bell pepper, cut into 6 pieces
1	large red bell pepper, cut into 6 pieces
1	large onion, chopped
3	large garlic cloves, minced
2	tablespoons sweet paprika
1	tablespoon ground cumin
¼	teaspoon saffron threads
3	tablespoons all-purpose flour
1	cup chicken broth
1	cup dry red wine
1	can (14.5 ounces) crushed tomatoes
2	cans (about 16 ounces each) chickpeas, drained
1½	teaspoons finely grated zest and the juice from 1 large orange

Adjust oven rack to lower-middle position and heat oven to 450 degrees. Heat a heavy soup kettle or a 5- to 6-quart Dutch oven over low heat. Meanwhile, place meat cubes and 1 tablespoon oil in a medium bowl and turn to coat. Season generously with salt and pepper.

A few minutes before cooking, add 1 tablespoon oil to pot and increase heat to a strong medium-high until wisps of smoke start to rise from the pan. Add peppers and cook, stirring, until lightly browned and crisp tender, about 3 minutes. Remove from pot; set aside.

Working in 2 batches, add meat and sear, turning only once, until 2 sides form an impressive, dark brown crust, 5 to 6 minutes per batch. Transfer to a bowl; set aside.

Add remaining 1 tablespoon oil to the hot empty pot, add onion, and cook, stirring, until softened, 4 to 5 minutes. Add garlic, paprika, cumin, and saffron and cook, stirring, until fragrant, about a minute. Whisk in flour, then broth, wine, and tomatoes, seasoning with salt and pepper.

Return beef to pot. Using two potholders to protect hands, place a sheet of heavy-duty foil over pot, pressing foil down so that it touches stew. Seal foil completely around edges. Place lid snugly on pot and cook until juices bubble. Set pot in oven and cook for 1½ hours.

Remove pot from oven and set over low heat. Carefully remove foil and stir in peppers, chickpeas, orange zest and juice, and a little water, if necessary, to make gravy. Remembering that pot and lid are hot, re-cover pot and simmer to blend flavors, about 5 minutes. Serve.

DRINK **A toasty medium-bodied Rioja Crianza**

Sautéed Chorizo Bites
with Sweet and Sour Fig Sauce

SERVES 6 TO 8

Establish the dinner's Spanish feel from the beginning with slices of sautéed chorizo, a spicy smoked dried sausage available in most supermarkets. Served with a delightful fig sauce, it's almost as quick as the instant alternative.

Add a wedge of Manchego, a semihard Spanish sheep's milk cheese, and the sausage will easily serve 8. If not serving the cheese, increase the sausage to 10 ounces for 8 people.

1 teaspoon olive oil

1 package (7 ounces) Spanish chorizo sausage (found with the sausages in many supermarkets)

¼ cup fig preserves (found in the jams and jellies section)

2 teaspoons Dijon mustard

Heat oil over medium heat in a medium skillet. Add sausage, reduce heat to low, and cook, turning once, until lightly browned and fat renders, 5 to 7 minutes. Transfer to a cutting board and slice diagonally ¼ inch thick.

Meanwhile, mix preserves and mustard in a microwave-safe cup and microwave until hot, about 30 seconds. Set dipping sauce on cutting board with sausage slices and serve with toothpicks.

INSTANT ALTERNATIVE: Set out a wedge of Manchego cheese, along with quince paste (found in the international aisle of supermarkets or in specialty cheese shops) as an accompaniment. If you can't find quince paste, look for pear or plum paste, an equally good match, or even firm fig preserves.

SALAD Baby Greens with Pimento-Stuffed Olives, Celery, and Toasted Almonds

SERVES 8

The pungent olives and toasted almonds in this salad reinforce the meal's Spanish feel. If you wish, you can substitute ¾ cup Lemon-Shallot Vinaigrette (page 234) for the dressing here.

10	ounces (about 15 cups) prewashed mixed baby greens
1¼	cups coarsely chopped pimento-stuffed olives
3	large celery stalks, chopped (1 heaping cup)
½	cup chopped roasted almonds
6–8	tablespoons extra-virgin olive oil
	Salt and freshly ground black pepper
1½–2	tablespoons sherry vinegar

Place greens, olives, celery, and almonds in a large bowl. Just before serving, toss with 6 tablespoons olive oil and a generous sprinkling of salt and pepper. Taste, adding more oil, salt, or pepper, if necessary. Add 1 ½ tablespoons vinegar and toss to coat, adding more, if necessary, to taste, and serve.

Creamy Flan

SERVES 8

Neufchâtel adds body to this quickly made, do-ahead flan, while evaporated and sweetened condensed milk offer incredible creaminess, all without unnecessary calories. Covered and refrigerated, the flan can be made up to 3 days ahead.

1 **cup sugar**

1 **package (8 ounces) light cream cheese (Neufchâtel), softened**

4 **large eggs**

1 **can (12 ounces) evaporated milk**

1 **can (14 ounces) sweetened condensed milk**

1 **teaspoon vanilla extract**

Adjust oven rack to middle position and heat oven to 325 degrees. Bring 1 quart water to a boil for a water bath.

Whisking constantly, bring sugar and ¼ cup water to a boil over medium heat in a medium heavy-bottomed saucepan. When mixture starts to boil, turn heat to medium-low and stop whisking. Continue to simmer until mixture turns golden brown, 10 to 15 minutes. Pour mixture into a 9-inch deep-dish pie plate set in a roasting pan large enough to accommodate it.

Meanwhile, beat cream cheese in a large bowl with an electric mixer until light and fluffy. Add eggs, one at a time, scraping down sides after each addition. Beat in evaporated and condensed milk and vanilla until smooth.

Set roasting pan in oven and pour flan mixture into pie plate. Pour in enough hot water to come about halfway up side of pie plate. Bake until flan is jiggly but set, about 1 hour. Remove from oven, cool to room temperature, and refrigerate until ready to serve. Run a small knife around perimeter of flan to loosen sides. Invert onto a large lipped platter. Cut into wedges and serve.

INSTANT ALTERNATIVE: Serve goblets of Dulce de Leche Ice Cream or top premium vanilla ice cream (1½ pints for 6 people) with a good store-bought caramel sauce.

Carnita-Style Beef

WITH ROASTED PEPPERS AND ONIONS

If you're looking for a vibrant, assemble-your-own kind of meal, stop right here. Omit the peppers and onions, if you like, but they're easy to prepare and can be roasted at any time while the beef braises, and they add color, crunch, and bulk to the rich beef.

APPETIZER Tortilla Chips with Shrimp Ceviche Dip
Instant Alternative: Tortilla Chips with Perked-Up Salsa

SALAD Cabbage Slaw with Radishes, Cilantro, and Scallions

DESSERT Warm Bananas Foster Tart
Instant Alternative: Baked Bananas Foster

Carnita-Style Beef
with Roasted Peppers and Onions

SERVES 8, WITH LEFTOVERS

By sealing the beef in the pan with heavy-duty foil and roasting it at a high temperature, you are essentially using your oven like a pressure cooker. You can halve the carnita recipe and braise a single roast in a large Dutch oven or soup kettle—but why would you? It's just as easy to braise two roasts as one, and the leftover shredded beef refrigerates well for several days and freezes too, making it perfect for a second meal. If halving the recipe, remember to roast the peppers and onions on a smaller baking sheet. Serve flour tortillas, not corn, with the beef.

2	boneless chuck roasts, 2½–3 pounds each
6	tablespoons olive oil, divided
2	tablespoons plus 2 teaspoons ground cumin, divided
	Salt and freshly ground black pepper
2	cans (4.5 ounces each) chopped green chiles, undrained
¼	cup chili powder
2	teaspoons dried oregano
8	large garlic cloves, minced
1	quart chicken broth
3	large onions, ends left intact, peeled, each cut into 12 wedges
3	large multicolored bell peppers, each cut into 12 wedges
24	medium flour tortillas
1	container (16 ounces) light or regular sour cream
	Fresh cilantro sprigs
2	limes, cut into wedges

Adjust oven racks to lowest and middle positions and heat oven to 450 degrees. Heat a large heavy roasting pan over two burners on low heat.

Meanwhile, place roasts in a large bowl, coat with 2 tablespoons oil, and season with 2 tablespoons cumin and a generous sprinkling of salt and pepper. Mix chiles, chili powder, remaining 2 teaspoons cumin, and oregano in a small bowl.

A few minutes before searing, increase heat to a strong medium high until wisps of smoke start to rise from pan. Add roasts and sear, turning only once, until both sides form an impressive brown crust, about 8 minutes total. Transfer roasts to a plate; set aside. Add garlic to pan and cook, stirring, until fragrant and golden, about 30 seconds. Add chile mixture and cook, stirring, to intensify flavor, another 30 seconds. Add chicken broth, bring to a simmer, and return roasts and any juices on plate to pan.

Using two potholders to protect hands, place a sheet of heavy-duty foil over pan, pressing down on foil so that it touches roasts. Seal foil around edges and repeat with a second sheet of foil to seal completely. Continue cooking on medium-high until juices bubble. Set pan on middle oven rack and cook for a total of 1 hour and 45 minutes.

Meanwhile, about 30 minutes before roasts are done, toss onions and peppers with remaining ¼ cup oil and sprinkle generously with salt and pepper. Spread on a baking sheet, place on bottom oven rack, cook until crisp-tender, about 30 minutes.

When roasts are done, remove from oven, cool, and shred meat into bite-size pieces.

Set peppers, onions, and meat aside, covered, in a warm place, while you cook tortillas.

You can microwave the tortillas, but I prefer to oven-steam them. Lower oven temperature to 350 degrees. Lay a damp paper towel on a 24-by-18-inch piece of heavy-duty foil. Set 2 stacks of 4 flour tortillas each side by side on towel. Cover with another damp paper towel and seal foil completely. Make 2 more packages in same manner. Warm in oven until steamy, about 5 minutes.

Place meat, peppers, and onions on a platter and serve with warm tortillas, bowls of sour cream, cilantro sprigs, and lime wedges.

DRINK For the shrimp, a clean fresh white, like Spanish Albariño, and for the carnitas, Zinfandel or Monastrell, a big, mellow contemporary Spanish red

Tortilla Chips with Shrimp Ceviche Dip

MAKES ABOUT 2½ CUPS

Although it requires a little dicing, slicing, chopping, and juicing, this dip is quite simple to mix and serve. Leftover dip is certainly fine a day or so later (the lime juice keeps the avocado from dramatic discoloration), but like guacamole, it has a brighter flavor and fresher look when made just a few hours before serving.

1   **pound cooked salad shrimp, whole if tiny, chopped if large**

½   **medium seedless cucumber, chopped**

1   **avocado, pitted, peeled, and cut into small dice**

4   **medium scallions, thinly sliced**

⅓   **cup chopped fresh cilantro**

½   **cup ketchup**

1   **tablespoon hot red pepper sauce**

¼   **cup fresh lime juice (from 1–2 limes)**

2   **tablespoons extra-virgin olive oil**

Taste-Like-Fried Tortillas (page 154) or one 14- to 16-ounce bag store-bought tortilla chips

Mix all ingredients except tortillas in a medium bowl. Cover and refrigerate. Serve with tortillas or tortilla chips for dipping.

INSTANT ALTERNATIVE: Serve Perked-Up Salsa with homemade or store-bought tortilla chips. You may never mistake store-bought salsa for fresh, but you can certainly perk up the jarred variety. Check out your local brands; my favorite nationally distributed brand is Pace. Empty a 16-ounce jar of salsa into a medium bowl. Stir in 3 to 4 tablespoons chopped fresh cilantro and 1 tablespoon fresh lime juice. Serve.

SALAD Cabbage Slaw with Radishes, Cilantro, and Scallions

SERVES 8

A simple crisp slaw is perfect with the spicy beef. You can skip the salad or simply toss the cabbage and radishes with olive oil and fresh lime juice.

1	pound shredded cabbage or a 1-pound package coleslaw mix
8	radishes, trimmed and thinly sliced
3	scallions, trimmed and thinly sliced
¼	cup chopped fresh cilantro
6–8	tablespoons olive oil
	Salt and freshly ground black pepper
1½–2	tablespoons fresh lime juice

Place cabbage, radishes, scallions, and cilantro in a large bowl. Just before serving, toss with 6 tablespoons olive oil and a generous sprinkling of salt and pepper. Taste, adding more oil, salt, or pepper, if necessary. Add 1½ tablespoons lime juice and toss to coat, adding more, if necessary, to taste, and serve.

Warm Bananas Foster Tart

SERVES 8 TO 12

You can prepare and refrigerate the tart several hours ahead and bake it during dinner. Or you can bake it a few hours ahead and warm it in a 400-degree oven for 5 to 7 minutes.

The bananas will be less likely to break when you are cutting them if you halve them crosswise first, and then slice the halves lengthwise.

If you forget to thaw the puff pastry sheet in advance, speed the thawing by microwaving the folded sheet for 15 seconds on high power. The sheet will be ready to unfold and roll in about 10 minutes. You can use either a metal or a Pyrex pan for this dessert, but it's much easier to invert the lighter-weight metal.

1 **stick (8 tablespoons) unsalted butter**
8 **ripe bananas, peeled and halved lengthwise (see headnote)**
3 **tablespoons dark rum**
1½ **cups packed dark brown sugar**
1 **sheet frozen puff pastry (from a 17.3-ounce box), thawed**
Premium vanilla ice cream (optional, but recommended)

Adjust oven rack to lowest position and heat oven to 400 degrees.

Place butter in a 13-by-9-inch pan (see headnote) and set in oven to melt. Meanwhile, gently toss bananas with rum. Remove pan from oven, sprinkle brown sugar over butter, arrange banana pieces in a single layer over pan bottom, and lay any remaining pieces on top.

Roll puff pastry sheet into 13-by-9-inch rectangle; lay over banana slices. Bake until pastry is golden brown, about 30 minutes. Immediately and carefully invert tart onto a serving platter or rimmed baking sheet. Cut into pieces and serve with a scoop of ice cream, if desired.

> **INSTANT ALTERNATIVE:** You can bake the butter, bananas, rum, and sugar, uncovered, in a 400-degree oven until juices are thick and bubbly, about 30 minutes. Serve warm with premium vanilla ice cream.

Braised Salmon

WITH FINGERLING POTATOES, SHALLOTS, AND ASPARAGUS

Here's a good choice for a chilly spring night when there's little time to prepare dinner. If you'd like to add a salad to this meal, consider Deviled Eggs on Butter Lettuce with Honey-Mustard Dressing (page 180). Keep this dish bright, beautiful, and evenly cooked by braising in two steps: the sturdier root vegetables first, followed by the more delicate salmon and asparagus.

APPETIZER Mini Parmesan Muffins with Prosciutto and Basil
Instant Alternative: Warm Savory Pluck-It Bread with Herbed Dipping Butter

DESSERT Lemon Meringue Puff Pastries
Instant Alternative: Lemon Mousse with Pizzelles and Fresh Raspberries

Braised Salmon
with Fingerling Potatoes, Shallots, and Asparagus

SERVES 6

If not making this dish in one session, get a head start by boiling the potatoes, carrots, and shallots and keeping them warm in a 170-degree oven for an hour or more. Or cook them even earlier and hold them, covered, at room temperature, then warm them in the oven as you heat the broth and clam juice to cook the salmon and asparagus. If you can find only thin asparagus, cook it after, rather than with, the salmon, until bright green and tender-crisp, 3 to 4 minutes. Toss any leftovers into a salad for tomorrow's lunch.

6 center-cut salmon fillets (2–2½ pounds)

   Salt and freshly ground black pepper

1 quart chicken broth

4 bottles (8 ounces each) clam juice

6 medium carrots, peeled and left whole

6 large shallots, peeled and left whole

1½ pounds fingerling potatoes or small red new potatoes

1½ pounds (about 1½ bunches) thick asparagus, tough ends snapped off

1½ teaspoons fresh lemon juice, plus lemon wedges for serving

Heat oven to 170 degrees. Sprinkle flesh side of salmon with salt and pepper.

Bring chicken broth, clam juice, carrots, shallots, and potatoes to a boil in a large heavy roasting pan set over two burners. Cover pan with a sheet of heavy-duty foil, reduce heat to low, and continue to cook until vegetables are just tender, about 15 minutes. Transfer vegetables to a large ovenproof platter; keep warm in oven. Add salmon fillets and asparagus (see headnote) to broth; cover and simmer until asparagus is just tender and salmon fillets are just opaque throughout (5 minutes for thin fillets and 7 minutes for thick fillets). Transfer to platter in oven. Stir lemon juice into broth and pour into a large Pyrex measuring cup, adding water, if necessary, to equal 2 cups. Heat broth in microwave and divide salmon and vegetables among six soup plates. Ladle hot broth over each portion and serve with lemon wedges

DRINK A sparkling wine to start, then a Pouilly-Fumé or other Sauvignon Blanc

APPETIZER # Mini Parmesan Muffins with Prosciutto and Basil

MAKES 4 DOZEN

Meat and cheese are baked right into savory mini muffins. If you prefer, serve the muffins in a breadbasket alongside the salmon. To make regular-size muffins, use a 12-cup (½-cup capacity) muffin tin. Reduce the oven temperature to 375 degrees and increase the baking time to 25 minutes. Warm leftovers in a 300- to 325-degree toaster oven.

- 3 **cups bleached all-purpose flour**
- 1 **tablespoon baking powder**
- ½ **teaspoon baking soda**
- 1 **teaspoon salt**
- 1 **cup finely grated Parmesan cheese (about 3 ounces)**
- ½ **cup minced prosciutto (about 2 ounces)**
- 1 **tablespoon dried basil**
- 1¼ **sticks (10 tablespoons) unsalted butter, softened**
- 2 **teaspoons sugar**
- 1 **tablespoon Dijon mustard**
- 2 **large eggs**
- 1½ **cups plain low-fat yogurt**

Adjust oven rack to lower-middle position and heat oven to 450 degrees. Mix flour, baking powder, baking soda, salt, Parmesan, prosciutto, and basil in a medium bowl.

Beat butter and sugar in a large bowl with an electric mixer until light and fluffy. Whisk mustard and eggs together, then beat into butter mixture until it forms pea-size lumps.

Alternating between dry ingredients and yogurt, beat in one third at a time, just until batter is smooth. Spray four 12-cup mini muffin tins with vegetable-oil cooking spray. Divide batter evenly among the cups. (A spring-action mini ice cream scoop works well. Muffin cups will be full.) Bake until golden brown, about 12 minutes. Cool pans on a wire rack, remove muffins, and continue to cool or serve.

INSTANT ALTERNATIVE: Bake Warm Savory Pluck-It Bread with Herbed Dipping Butter. Adjust oven rack to lower-middle position and heat oven to 450 degrees. Cut a 1-pound ball pizza dough into 50 pieces (a bench knife or dough scraper works well for this). Arrange pieces close together in 2 circular rows around a 12-inch pizza pan to form a wreath shape. Bake until golden brown, 12 to 15 minutes. Meanwhile, for dipping butter, whisk ½ stick (4 tablespoons) softened butter, 2 tablespoons olive oil, 1 minced large garlic clove, 2 tablespoons minced fresh parsley, and ¼ teaspoon each salt and freshly ground black pepper. Serve warm bread with dipping butter.

Lemon Meringue Puff Pastries

SERVES 6

Frozen puff pastry shells take the place of piecrust here, making it possible to enjoy a variation on an all-American favorite—lemon meringue pie—in less than half an hour. If you plan to serve the tarts soon after baking, omit the cornstarch mixture in the meringue, which prevents it from developing beads of moisture over time. If adding the cornstarch mixture, however, make sure it's warm when beating it into the meringue. Otherwise, it might cause the meringue to lump.

- ½ **cup plus 6 tablespoons sugar, divided**
- 3 **tablespoons cornstarch, divided**
  Pinch salt
- 3 **large eggs, separated**
- 1½ **teaspoons finely grated lemon zest**
- ¼ **cup fresh lemon juice**
- 1 **tablespoon butter**
- ½ **teaspoon vanilla extract**
- 1 **box (10 ounces) frozen puff pastry shells, baked and hollowed as directed on package**

Adjust oven rack to lower-middle position and heat oven to 325 degrees. Whisk ½ cup sugar, 2 tablespoons cornstarch, and salt together in a medium nonreactive saucepan. Add yolks and immediately but gradually whisk in ¾ cup water. Bring mixture to a simmer over medium heat, whisking occasionally at the beginning and more frequently as mixture begins to thicken, 4 to 5 minutes. Whisk in lemon zest, then juice, and finally butter. Whisking constantly, simmer filling for 1 minute. Remove from heat and place plastic wrap on surface to prevent a skin from forming.

Meanwhile, heat remaining 1 tablespoon cornstarch and ⅓ cup water over low heat in a small saucepan, whisking occasionally, then more frequently as mixture thickens and turns translucent; remove from heat. Immediately beat egg whites with vanilla in a medium bowl with an electric mixer until frothy. Beat remaining 6 tablespoons sugar into egg whites, 1 tablespoon at a time, until soft peaks form. Dollop warm cornstarch mixture into meringue and continue to beat to stiff peaks.

Spoon a portion of warm lemon filling into each prepared pastry shell and top with meringue. Bake until meringue is golden brown, about 15 minutes. Transfer to a wire rack and cool to warm or room temperature. Serve.

INSTANT ALTERNATIVE: Make Lemon Mousse with Pizzelles and Fresh Raspberries. The assembly of this dessert is last-minute but quick, and the mousse can be made a day ahead. If raspberries aren't available or are too pricey, substitute blueberries or lightly sugared sliced strawberries.

Whisk ⅔ cup jarred lemon curd with ½ teaspoon finely grated lemon zest. Beat 1 cup heavy cream in a medium bowl with an electric mixer to stiff peaks. Stir ½ cup whipped cream into lemon curd to soften, then fold in remaining whipped cream. Just before serving, lay 1 pizzelle on each of six dessert plates (you need 12 pizzelles; you can find them in the bakery department or cookie aisle of the grocery store). Top each with a portion of mousse. Stand a second pizzelle straight up in the mousse. Garnish with raspberries (½ cup total) and serve, letting people use the cookies as a spoon.

Braised Rack of Lamb
WITH CARROTS, POTATOES, AND SPINACH

Rack of lamb and spinach, braised with shallots, carrots, and potatoes, is perfect for an elegant yet on-the-fly Saint Patrick's Day celebration.

APPETIZER Irish Soda Bread with Smoked Salmon and Lemon-Dill Butter
Instant Alternative: Smoked Salmon Bites with Lemon-Dill Butter

DESSERT Sugar-Rimmed Mugs of Irish Coffee
Instant Alternative: Chocolate–Chocolate Mint Cookie Ice Cream

Braised Rack of Lamb
with Carrots, Potatoes, and Spinach

SERVES 6 TO 8

You can make most of this dish ahead: Sear the lamb and set it aside; cook the vegetables (except the spinach) and arrange them on an ovenproof platter, cover loosely with foil, and keep them warm in a 170-degree oven for up to an hour. About 20 minutes before serving, add a couple of cups of water to the roasting pan, bring it to a simmer, and add the lamb.

If you prefer larger racks of lamb, increase the cooking time by 3 to 5 minutes, keeping track of the internal temperature. And if you're serving big eaters, you may want to throw an extra rack in the pan.

You can make the drizzle several hours ahead, if using.

2 small racks of lamb (about 1 pound each)

Salt and freshly ground black pepper

1 teaspoon sugar

2 tablespoons vegetable or olive oil

8 medium carrots, peeled and cut into large chunks

8 large shallots, peeled and left whole

2 quarts chicken broth

2 pounds fingerling potatoes or small red new potatoes

2 pounds prewashed spinach

PARSLEY-MINT DRIZZLE (OPTIONAL)

½ cup chopped fresh parsley

½ cup chopped fresh mint

6 thinly sliced cornichons or baby dill pickles, plus 1 teaspoon pickle juice

¼ cup drained capers

2 scallions, thinly sliced

¼ cup extra-virgin olive oil

Salt and freshly ground black pepper

Set a large heavy roasting pan over two burners on low heat. Meanwhile, season the racks generously with salt and pepper to taste and sugar.

A couple of minutes before cooking, increase heat to a strong medium-high until wisps of smoke start to rise from pan. Turn on exhaust fan and add lamb, searing on 3 sides: fat side down, fat side up (to sear meaty section of bone side) and, finally, rack up (to sear meaty bottom), about 1 minute per side. Transfer to a plate and set aside. Add oil to pan, then add carrots and shallots and cook, stirring, until well browned, about 5 minutes.

Add broth and potatoes and bring to a boil. Add lamb and reduce heat to medium. Using two potholders to protect hands, cover pan with heavy-duty foil and seal all around. Continue to cook until vegetables are just tender and the thickest part of the lamb registers 130 degrees on a meat thermometer, 15 to 18 minutes.

Parsley-Mint Drizzle: Meanwhile, if you're serving the drizzle, mix the parsley, mint, cornichons and juice, capers, scallions, oil, and salt and pepper to taste in a small bowl.

Arrange vegetables and lamb on a large platter and cover loosely. Add spinach to simmering broth; cook until just wilted, 3 to 4 minutes; arrange on platter. Pour broth into a heatproof pitcher. To serve, carve lamb into chops and divide, along with vegetables, among soup plates. Pour hot broth over each portion and serve with Parsley-Mint Drizzle, if desired.

DRINK **If it's Saint Patrick's Day, beer, or, for wine, a good Cabernet or Bordeaux**

APPETIZER # Irish Soda Bread with Smoked Salmon and Lemon-Dill Butter

SERVES 8

The dough for this soda bread comes together in about five minutes—faster than most ovens take to preheat—and bakes as you make the main course. Set out the remaining ingredients and let your guests assemble their own appetizer.

You can also serve this as a first course, arranging sliced bread and smoked salmon on small plates, with a smear of softened lemon-dill butter and sprigs of fresh dill alongside. If there's leftover bread, enjoy it toasted for breakfast.

SODA BREAD

3½ cups bleached all-purpose flour

1½ teaspoons salt

1½ teaspoons sugar

¾ teaspoon baking soda

1½ cups buttermilk

FLAVORED BUTTER

½ stick (4 tablespoons) unsalted butter, softened

2 tablespoons minced fresh dill

½ teaspoon finely grated lemon zest

1 teaspoon fresh lemon juice

1 small scallion, thinly sliced

Salt and freshly ground black pepper

8 ounces sliced smoked salmon

Soda Bread: Adjust oven rack to lower-middle position and heat oven to 450 degrees. Mix flour, salt, sugar, and baking soda in a large, wide bowl. Add buttermilk and stir with a fork until dough resembles small tatters of cloth. Using hands, briefly knead dough in bowl to form a roughly 8-inch ball. Place dough on a small baking pan, slashing top with a cross or an X. Bake until bread starts to turn golden, about 10 minutes. Reduce oven temperature to 400 degrees and continue to bake until bread is crisp and golden brown, about 35 minutes longer. Transfer to a wire rack and cool slightly.

Flavored Butter: Meanwhile, mix butter, dill, lemon zest, juice, scallion, and salt and pepper to taste in a small bowl.

Just before serving, slice a couple of slices off loaf and place bread, salmon, and bowl of lemon-dill butter on a large cutting board and invite your guests to help themselves.

INSTANT ALTERNATIVE: Make Smoked Salmon Bites. Cut 4 mini bagels in half crosswise and cut a thin slice off each rounded bottom and top to stabilize slices. Make lemon-dill butter (see opposite) and spread a portion over one side of each bagel half. Top with smoked salmon slices and cut into bite-size hors d'oeuvres, garnishing each with a small fresh dill sprig. Save leftover bagels for tomorrow's breakfast, lunch, or nibble.

Or just set a basket of mini bagels on a cutting board with smoked salmon and a little dish of lemon-dill butter.

DESSERT # Sugar-Rimmed Mugs of Irish Coffee

SERVES 8

For the Irish coffee, you can sugar the rims and whip the cream several hours ahead. After that, it's just pour, spike, dollop, and serve.

1   teaspoon plus 8 jiggers (1½ cups) Irish whiskey, divided

¾   cup sugar, divided

8   cups hot strong brewed coffee (regular or decaffeinated)

1   cup heavy cream, whipped to firm peaks

Pour 1 teaspoon whiskey onto a small plate and ¼ cup sugar onto a second small plate. Dip the rim of each of eight coffee mugs into whiskey, then sugar to coat completely; set aside.

Just before serving, carefully pour hot coffee into mugs (try not to disturb sugared rims). Stir 1 jigger (3 tablespoons) whiskey and 1 tablespoon sugar into each coffee mug. Top with a dollop of whipped cream and serve immediately.

> **INSTANT ALTERNATIVE:** Make your own Chocolate–Chocolate Mint Cookie Ice Cream. Crush 16 chocolate mint cookies, such as Oreos or Pepperidge Farm Milanos, in a quart-size freezer bag with a rolling pin. Microwave 1 quart premium chocolate ice cream (avoid chocolate–chocolate chip flavors because the bits of frozen chocolate compete with the cookie) to soften slightly, about 30 seconds. Turn into a large bowl and break up with a wooden spoon or spatula. Fold crushed cookies into ice cream until well incorporated. Return to freezer. Just before serving, spoon ice cream into eight goblets and garnish each with a fresh mint sprig.

Lamb and Potato Stew
WITH LEMON AND DILL

A riff on the classic veal stew *blanquette de veau,* this light, colorful meal is perfect for a cool spring evening. Since the lamb chunks aren't seared before stewing, this dish assembles quickly and cooks in a mere hour and a half.

APPETIZER Buttermilk Biscuit Bites with Feta and Sun-Dried Tomatoes
Instant Alternative: Spicy Marinated Feta Cubes with Warm Pita

SALAD Greens with Eggs, Peas, Scallions, and Mint

DESSERT Light Vanilla Panna Cotta with Sugared Balsamic Strawberries
Instant Alternative: Sour Cream–Capped Yogurt with Sugared Balsamic Strawberries

Lamb and Potato Stew
with Lemon and Dill

SERVES 8

Although you'll probably want to make this stew early (up to 3 days ahead and gently reheated works well), be sure to preserve its bright color and flavor by adding the lemon zest and dill just before serving. For a richer, darker stew, sear the meat before stewing. Not sure everyone likes lamb? Substitute boneless pork shoulder.

¼ **cup olive oil, divided**

6 **large garlic cloves, minced**

2 **tablespoons minced fresh rosemary or 2 teaspoons Italian seasoning**

¼ **cup all-purpose flour**

2 **cups chicken broth**

¾ **cup dry vermouth or white wine**

¼ **cup fresh lemon juice (from 1–2 lemons)**

3 **pounds lamb shoulder or leg, cut into 1½- to 2-inch cubes**

6 **medium carrots (about 1 pound), peeled and cut into medium chunks**

8 **ounces frozen pearl onions (scant 2 cups), not thawed**

6 **red new potatoes (about 1 pound), quartered**

Salt and freshly ground black pepper

¼ **cup minced fresh dill**

2 **teaspoons finely grated lemon zest**

Adjust oven racks to lowest and middle positions and heat oven to 450 degrees.

Heat 2 tablespoons oil, garlic, and rosemary over medium-high heat in a 5- to 6-quart Dutch oven or soup kettle. When garlic starts to turn golden and mix is fragrant, whisk in flour, then broth, vermouth, and lemon juice. Bring to a simmer, add lamb, and return to a simmer.

Using two potholders to protect hands, place a sheet of heavy-duty foil over pot, pressing foil down so that it just touches stew, and seal foil tightly around edges. Place lid snugly on pot and heat stew until you hear juices bubble. Transfer to oven and bake until meat is tender, about 1½ hours.

After 45 minutes, toss carrots, frozen pearl onions, and potatoes in a 13-by-9-inch pan with remaining 2 tablespoons oil and a sprinkling of salt and pepper. Set on bottom rack in oven and roast until vegetables are tender, about 45 minutes longer. Remove stew and vegetables from oven. Remembering that pot and lid are hot, stir vegetables, along with dill and lemon zest, into stew; bring to a simmer over medium heat. Simmer to heat through and blend flavors, about 5 minutes. Serve.

DRINK   A dry Sauvignon Blanc with the appetizer and with the stew, a lighter-style Côtes du Rhône or other Grenache-based red wine

APPETIZER Buttermilk Biscuit Bites with Feta and Sun-Dried Tomatoes

MAKES 30

Although the biscuits are best baked just before serving, the dry ingredients, with the butter grated in, can be measured and frozen and the wet ingredients can be whisked together and refrigerated up to a day ahead. About a half hour before serving, heat the oven, mix the wet ingredients into the dry, pinch off dough balls, and bake. Any leftover biscuits can be toasted for tomorrow's breakfast or served as an accompaniment to a bowl of soup.

2 **cups bleached all-purpose flour**

2 **teaspoons baking powder**

¼ **teaspoon baking soda**

¾ **teaspoon salt**

¾ **cup crumbled feta cheese (generous 4 ounces)**

1 **teaspoon dried oregano**

1 **stick (8 tablespoons) unsalted butter, frozen solid**

2 **tablespoons minced sun-dried tomatoes packed in oil**

1 **cup cold buttermilk, plus a few more teaspoons if necessary**

Adjust oven rack to middle position and heat oven to 450 degrees. Line a baking sheet with a Silpat baking mat or parchment paper or spray the baking sheet with vegetable-oil cooking spray.

Mix flour, baking powder, baking soda, salt, feta, and oregano with a fork in a medium bowl. Using a box grater, coarsely grate frozen butter into the dry ingredients and mix quickly with fingertips to blend evenly. With a fork, mix tomatoes into buttermilk. Continuing with the fork, mix buttermilk mixture into dry ingredients until dough just comes together, adding a little more buttermilk if necessary.

Pinch dough into 30 rough rounds, placing 6 rows of 5 biscuits each on the baking sheet. Bake until golden brown, 10 to 12 minutes. Serve.

> **INSTANT ALTERNATIVE:** Serve feta in oil and spices (usually packaged in a jar and located in the refrigerated cheese section of many grocery stores) with warm pitas (heat in a 350-degree oven for 4 to 5 minutes) for dipping in the oil and toothpicks for spearing the feta.

◼ SALAD ◼ Greens with Eggs, Peas, Scallions, and Mint

SERVES 8

With peas, mint, scallions, and boiled eggs, this salad underscores the meal's fresh spring feel. You can use ¾ cup Lemon-Shallot Vinaigrette (page 234) in place of the dressing here, if you'd rather.

10	**ounces (about 15 cups) prewashed mixed baby greens**
3	**boiled eggs (see headnote on page 180), diced**
3–4	**scallions, thinly sliced**
⅔	**cup frozen peas, thawed**
¼	**cup chopped fresh mint**
6–8	**tablespoons extra-virgin olive oil**
	Salt and freshly ground black pepper
1½–2	**tablespoons fresh lemon juice**

Place greens, eggs, scallions, peas, and mint in a large bowl. Just before serving, toss with 6 tablespoons olive oil and a generous sprinkling of salt and pepper. Taste, adding more oil, salt, or pepper, if necessary. Add 1½ tablespoons lemon juice; toss to coat, adding more, if necessary, to taste, and serve.

Light Vanilla Panna Cotta with Sugared Balsamic Strawberries

SERVES 8

Evaporated milk is a wonderful, lighter alternative to heavy cream in rich desserts. Panna cotta is no exception. You can make and refrigerate these desserts up to 2 or 3 days ahead. Just remember to put plastic wrap directly over the surface to prevent a skin from forming.

- 2 **cans (12 ounces each) evaporated milk**
- ¾ **cup sugar, divided**
- 1 **envelope unflavored gelatin**
- 1½ **teaspoons vanilla extract**
- 1 **pint strawberries, hulled and sliced**
- 1 **tablespoon balsamic vinegar**

Coat eight custard cups with vegetable-oil cooking spray and set in two 9-inch baking pans.

Whisk milk, ½ cup sugar, and gelatin in a medium saucepan until gelatin softens and sugar dissolves. Bring milk mixture to a simmer over medium heat. Remove from heat and stir in vanilla. Divide mixture among prepared cups. Cover baking pans with plastic wrap and refrigerate until desserts are set, at least 4 hours and preferably overnight.

Mix strawberries with vinegar and remaining ¼ cup sugar in a medium bowl. Let stand until juicy, 30 minutes to 2 hours.

Just before serving, run a thin-bladed knife around perimeter of custard cups. Turn each panna cotta out onto a small dessert plate, spoon a portion of sauce around it, and serve.

INSTANT ALTERNATIVE: Serve Sour Cream–Capped Yogurt with Sugared Balsamic Strawberries, one of my favorite simple desserts. Spoon ½ cup Greek-style yogurt onto each of eight dessert plates. Stir 1½ cups sour cream to loosen, then top each yogurt mound with 3 tablespoons sour cream. Sprinkle each dessert with 2 teaspoons sugar and serve with Sugared Balsamic Strawberries alongside (see above).

Braised Lamb Shanks

WITH TOMATOES, AROMATIC VEGETABLES, AND WHITE BEANS

Braised lamb shanks are one of my family's top ten favorite fall and winter dishes. Call your grocery store's meat department ahead to make sure it has the shanks. The butcher can usually get them in with a day's notice. Once you've got the shanks, however, they're easy to cook.

Check out the ingredient list: You've probably got most of the ingredients in your kitchen right now. White beans keep this stew one-dish, but if you like, you can omit them and serve the shanks with mashed potatoes or polenta.

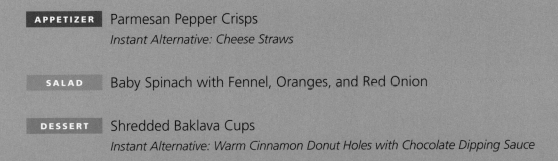

APPETIZER Parmesan Pepper Crisps
Instant Alternative: Cheese Straws

SALAD Baby Spinach with Fennel, Oranges, and Red Onion

DESSERT Shredded Baklava Cups
Instant Alternative: Warm Cinnamon Donut Holes with Chocolate Dipping Sauce

Braised Lamb Shanks

with Tomatoes, Aromatic Vegetables, and White Beans

SERVES 6

These braised shanks can be refrigerated for up to 3 days before serving. Reheat them over medium-low heat right in the roasting pan, covered with foil to hold in the heat.

- 6 large lamb shanks
- 2 tablespoons olive oil, plus 1 tablespoon if necessary
  Salt and freshly ground black pepper
- 1 large onion, chopped
- 3 large carrots, cut into medium chunks
- 3 celery stalks, cut into medium chunks
- 3 large garlic cloves, minced
- 1 tablespoon herbes de Provence or Italian seasoning
- 3 tablespoons all-purpose flour
- 2 cups chicken broth
- 1 cup dry red wine
- 1 can (14.5 ounces) crushed tomatoes
- 3 cans (about 16 ounces each) cannellini or other white beans, drained

Adjust oven rack to lower-middle position and heat oven to 450 degrees. Heat a large heavy roasting pan set over two burners on low heat. Meanwhile, place shanks in a medium bowl with 2 tablespoons oil and turn to coat. Season generously with salt and pepper.

A few minutes before searing shanks, increase heat to a strong medium-high until wisps of smoke rise from pan. Add shanks and sear on all sides until well browned, 7 to 8 minutes total. Transfer to a bowl. Shanks should have rendered enough fat to cook onion. If not, add another tablespoon of oil to pan.

Add onion, carrots, and celery to roasting pan and cook, stirring, until lightly browned, about 5 minutes. Add garlic and herbes de Provence and cook until fragrant, about 1 minute. Whisk in flour, then broth, wine, and tomatoes, and season with salt and pepper to taste.

Return shanks to pan. Using two potholders to protect hands, place a sheet of heavy-duty foil over pan. Press foil down so that it touches shanks and seal foil completely around edges.

Repeat with a second sheet of foil to ensure a tight seal. Continue to cook shanks on medium-high until you hear juices bubble. Set pan in oven and cook for 1½ hours.

Transfer pan from oven to stovetop. Arrange shanks on a serving platter and cover with foil to keep warm. Stir beans into pan juices (remembering that pan handles are hot) and simmer over two burners on medium heat to blend flavors, about 5 minutes. Serve.

DRINK A dry sparkling wine with the Parmesan crisps and a medium-bodied, dry Italian red—Barbera d'Asti or Barbera d'Alba—or an earthy red from Languedoc with the shanks

Parmesan Pepper Crisps

MAKES 1 DOZEN PER BAKING SHEET

These crisps are a festive start to nearly any dinner, so when you make them, always bake a few extra. They store well—a solid 2 weeks—in an airtight tin. Instead of black pepper, try sprinkling the crisps with dried thyme, herbes de Provence, or even a little cayenne pepper. Make multiple batches, as desired.

1 scant cup coarsely grated Parmesan cheese, preferably Parmigiano-Reggiano (the coarse holes of a box grater work well)

1 teaspoon freshly ground black pepper (see headnote)

Adjust oven rack to lower-middle position and heat oven to 350 degrees. Line a baking sheet with a Silpat baking mat or parchment paper.

Spoon a rounded tablespoon of cheese onto baking sheet, then spread into a round with fingertips so that cheese is more or less in a single layer. Repeat with remaining cheese, keeping disks about 1 inch apart (you should get about 12 wafers per sheet). Sprinkle with pepper.

Bake until crisps turn golden, about 8 minutes. Transfer crisps to a wire rack to cool.

INSTANT ALTERNATIVE: Pick up a package of cheese straws and, if you like, set out a bowl of mixed olives. If they're packed in brine, drain them and drizzle with olive oil.

Baby Spinach with Fennel, Oranges, and Red Onion

SERVES 6

This spinach salad is a cool, sweet contrast to the rich lamb shanks. You can toss the salad with ½ cup Orange Vinaigrette (page 18), if you like, instead of the oil and rice wine vinegar.

3	medium oranges
7	ounces (about 10 cups) prewashed baby spinach
½	medium fennel bulb, cored and thinly sliced
¼	medium red onion, thinly sliced
4–6	tablespoons extra-virgin olive oil
	Salt and freshly ground black pepper
1½–2	tablespoons rice wine vinegar

With a large knife, cut off tops and bottoms of oranges and stand on end Slicing along sides, cut off rind and pith using a small sharp knife. Working over a bowl to catch juice, slice between membranes to cut out segments.

Place spinach, orange segments and juice, fennel, and onion in a large bowl. Just before serving, toss with 4 tablespoons olive oil and a generous sprinkling of salt and pepper. Taste, adding more oil, salt, or pepper, if necessary. Add 1½ tablespoons vinegar; toss to coat, adding more, if necessary, to taste, and serve.

Shredded Baklava Cups

MAKES 1 DOZEN

These little baklava "nests" offer all the irresistible flavor of the popular Greek dessert without all the work. Just remove one of the phyllo rolls from the package and cut it crosswise into strips. Once the ribbons are unfurled and separated, they can be drizzled and tossed with butter—much simpler than the traditional layering method. The baklava cups can be wrapped in foil and stored at room temperature for a couple of days.

- 1 **8-ounce package (from a 16-ounce box) frozen phyllo dough, thawed**
- 1 **cup roasted pistachios, finely ground in a food processor, divided**
- 1 **teaspoon ground cinnamon**
- 1 **stick (8 tablespoons) unsalted butter, melted**
- 6 **tablespoons honey**
- 6 **tablespoons sugar**

Adjust oven rack to lower-middle position and heat oven to 350 degrees. Line 12 muffin tin cups with cupcake liners. Spray liners with vegetable-oil cooking spray. Leaving phyllo dough rolled up, cut crosswise into 1-inch-wide strips. Working with one 1-inch-wide section at a time, toss dough in a large bowl, separating strips to make phyllo ribbons. Repeat with remaining sections of dough. Add all but 2 tablespoons pistachios and cinnamon to phyllo strips and toss to coat. Drizzle one quarter butter evenly over ribbons; toss to coat. Repeat drizzling and tossing 3 more times with remaining butter. Fill each muffin cup with phyllo ribbons, pressing lightly to compress. Sprinkle cups with remaining 2 tablespoons pistachios. Bake until golden brown, 22 to 25 minutes.

Meanwhile, bring honey, sugar, and 6 tablespoons water to a boil in a medium saucepan. Set aside and cool to warm. Pour warm syrup over hot baklava cups. Let cool to room temperature and serve.

INSTANT ALTERNATIVE: Adjust oven rack to lower-middle position and heat oven to 325 degrees. Place 2 dozen cinnamon-flavored donut holes (purchased from a donut shop, if possible) on a baking sheet and bake until warm, about 5 minutes. Serve warm donuts with Warm Chocolate Dipping Sauce (see opposite).

Warm Chocolate Dipping Sauce

MAKES 2½ CUPS

Mix 1 tablespoon cornstarch with 1 tablespoon water. Heat 4 ounces bittersweet chocolate with 2 cups milk, ¼ cup sugar, and ¼ teaspoon instant espresso or coffee powder in a medium saucepan over medium heat. When chocolate melts, whisk in cornstarch mixture, bring to a simmer, and continue to simmer until chocolate milk thickens to dipping-sauce consistency, almost immediately. Serve warm.

Worldly Casseroles

Doable, Delicious Paella

Paella, the classic Spanish seafood, sausage, and rice dish, is guaranteed fun. Since there's such a variety of ingredients—sausage, chicken, shrimp, and scallops—this dish works well when you don't know your crowd's taste. You've got lots of latitude.

APPETIZER Baked Goat Cheese in Tomato-Olive Sauce with Toasted Baguette
Instant Alternative: Spanish Marcona Almonds

SALAD Mixed Greens with Gazpacho Vegetables

DESSERT Orange Sherbet with Hot Fudge Sauce

Doable, Delicious Paella

x4

SERVES 6

Although the ingredient list may look daunting, paella can be prepped up to 2 hours ahead to the point of adding the rice. Near dinner, stir in the rice, saffron, pepper flakes, broth, and tomatoes and cook, covered, for 20 (unattended) minutes. Stir in the shrimp, scallops, peas, and parsley and steam for a few minutes, until the seafood is just cooked. (If serving this at a sit-down dinner, simply stir in the seafood as guests begin their salad.) For a larger crowd, you can double the recipe and use a large heavy roasting pan set over two burners instead of a 12-inch skillet.

Leftovers make a great lunch or dinner—just warm them in the microwave.

1	pound (about 4 medium) boneless, skinless chicken thighs, cut into 2-inch pieces
2	tablespoons olive oil, divided
1½	teaspoons paprika
1	teaspoon dried oregano
	Salt and freshly ground black pepper
8	ounces cooked chorizo or linguiça sausages, sliced diagonally ½ inch thick
1	Spanish onion, chopped
½	large red bell pepper, chopped
3	large garlic cloves, peeled and smashed
1½	cups short- or medium-grain rice
	Pinch saffron threads
½	teaspoon crushed red pepper flakes
3	cups chicken broth
1	can (14.5 ounces) petite diced tomatoes, undrained
½	pound (16–20 count) peeled and deveined shrimp, preferably wild
½	pound bay scallops
½	cup frozen peas, thawed
¼	cup chopped fresh parsley leaves

Drizzle chicken with 1 tablespoon oil and sprinkle with paprika, oregano, and a generous sprinkling of salt and pepper; toss to coat.

Heat a large (11- to 12-inch) deep skillet over medium-high heat. When wisps of smoke start to rise from the pan, add chicken and cook until brown and just cooked through, 3 to 4 minutes per side. Transfer to a small bowl.

Add remaining 1 tablespoon oil and sausages and cook until well browned, 3 to 4 minutes. Add onion, bell pepper, and garlic and cook until tender, about 4 minutes longer. Stir in rice, saffron, and pepper flakes.

Add broth and tomatoes and continue cooking over medium-high heat until liquid simmers. Reduce heat to low, cover with lid or heavy-duty foil, and cook until most of the liquid is absorbed, about 15 minutes. Stir in chicken, shrimp, scallops and their juices, peas, and parsley and cook until seafood is cooked through, about 5 minutes longer. Turn off heat and let stand, covered, for a few minutes. Serve straight from the pan or transfer to a large platter, arranging seafood and chicken as desired.

DRINK For red, a young Rioja; for white, Verdejo; or a cool, crisp rosé

APPETIZER Baked Goat Cheese in Tomato-Olive Sauce with Toasted Baguette

SERVES 6

Although toasted baguette slices are especially nice with this appetizer, you can, in a pinch, serve sturdy flat-bread crackers or bruschetta toasts with it. The olive-studded tomato sauce simmers for a mere 10 minutes and can be made up to 5 days ahead and refrigerated. Or simply simmer the olives quickly in a good-quality store-bought marinara sauce, top with fresh goat cheese rounds, and bake. Warmed in the microwave, the baked goat cheese pairs nicely with a light lunch salad the next day.

1 tablespoon olive oil

2 garlic cloves, minced

Half a 28-ounce can crushed tomatoes

8 pitted kalamata olives, coarsely chopped

½ thin baguette, thinly sliced

2 small logs (about 3½ ounces each) goat cheese, sliced crosswise into ¾-inch-thick disks

Place oil and garlic in a saucepan over medium heat and cook until garlic starts to sizzle and turn golden. Add tomatoes and olives, bring to a simmer, reduce heat to medium-low, and continue to simmer until sauce is thick enough to mound on a spoon, 10 to 12 minutes.

About 30 minutes before serving, adjust oven rack to center position and heat oven to 450 degrees. Place baguette slices in a single layer on a wire rack; bake until golden brown, about 5 minutes. Arrange in a basket.

Pour tomato sauce into a small ovenproof pan and top with goat cheese disks. Bake until bubbly, about 10 minutes. Turn on broiler and cook until goat cheese lightly browns, 1 to 2 minutes longer. Serve with a knife, allowing guests to top their own toasts.

INSTANT ALTERNATIVE: Serve Spanish Marcona Almonds. Spanish Marcona almonds, which have been fried and lightly salted, are fatter, crunchier, and richer-tasting than ordinary almonds. They are available at gourmet stores and occasionally at larger supermarkets.

Mixed Greens with Gazpacho Vegetables

SERVES 6

Studded with traditional gazpacho soup vegetables—tomatoes, cucumbers, bell peppers, and onions—this light, fresh salad is a natural with the rich paella.

7	ounces (about 10 cups) prewashed mixed baby greens
2	plum tomatoes, cut into small dice and lightly salted
½	seedless English cucumber, cut into small dice and lightly salted
½	yellow bell pepper, stemmed, seeded, and cut into small dice
½	small red onion, cut into small dice
¼–½	cup extra-virgin olive oil
	Salt and freshly ground black pepper
1–1½	tablespoons sherry vinegar

Place greens, tomatoes, cucumber, bell pepper, and onion in a large bowl. Just before serving, toss with ¼ cup olive oil and a generous sprinkling of salt and pepper. Taste, adding more oil, salt, or pepper, if necessary. Add 1 tablespoon vinegar and toss to coat, adding more, if necessary, to taste, and serve.

Orange Sherbet with Hot Fudge Sauce

SERVES 6

This sherbet is so simple that it's essentially instant. You might have a little leftover chocolate sauce—never a bad thing! Pepperidge Farm Chocolate Fudge Pirouette cookies make an easy, attractive garnish.

1 can (14 ounces) sweetened condensed milk
2 ounces unsweetened chocolate
½ teaspoon instant coffee powder
1½ teaspoons vanilla extract
1 quart orange sherbet or sorbet

Heat condensed milk, chocolate, 6 tablespoons water, and coffee powder in a medium saucepan over medium heat, stirring frequently, then constantly, until sauce turns from grainy to creamy smooth. Remove from heat and stir in vanilla.

Spoon a portion of warm sauce into each of six goblets or bowls. Top with a portion of sherbet and serve.

One-Pot Penne

WITH TURKEY-FETA MEATBALLS

Meatless Delicious: One-Pot Penne with Spinach-Feta Balls

With potent ingredients like feta, garlic, and oregano flavoring the meatballs, lean ground turkey delivers all the satisfaction of ground beef. Feel free, however, to use a meatloaf mix.

Not only does cooking the pasta with the sauce save time and a pot, but the pasta actually tastes more flavorful.

APPETIZER Warm Tapenade
Instant Alternative: Olive Bar

SALAD Caesar Salad Flatbread Pizzas

DESSERT Chocolate-Hazelnut Ice Cream Sandwiches
Instant Alternative: Your Favorite Premium Ice Cream Confection

One-Pot Penne
with Turkey-Feta Meatballs

SERVES 6 TO 8

Up to the point of adding the water and cooking the pasta, the meatballs and sauce can be made up to 3 days ahead and stored in the refrigerator.

8   garlic cloves, peeled, 3 left whole, 5 minced

1½   pounds ground turkey (93% lean)

¾   cup crumbled feta cheese (generous 4 ounces), plus more for topping

½   cup crumbled saltine crackers (about 12 crackers)

½   teaspoon dried oregano

1¾   teaspoons salt, divided

1   large egg

1   tablespoon tomato paste

¼   cup olive oil

4   thin slices prosciutto (about 2 ounces), minced

1   cup dry red wine

2   cans (28 ounces each) crushed tomatoes

1   pound penne pasta

Heat a small skillet over medium-high heat. Add 3 whole garlic cloves and toast until spotty brown, about 5 minutes. Remove garlic from skillet, smash, and mince.

Meanwhile, break up ground turkey into a medium bowl. With a fork, mix in feta, cracker crumbs, oregano, and ¾ teaspoon salt. Mix egg, minced toasted garlic, and tomato paste together in a small bowl; stir into turkey mixture with fork until thoroughly combined. Using a 2-tablespoon measure, such as a coffee scoop, form mixture into about 36 cylindrical drum shapes.

Heat oil over low heat in a large heavy roasting pan set over two burners. A couple of minutes before frying meatballs, increase heat to medium-high. Add meatballs and cook, turning once, until browned on both sides, about 5 minutes total. Transfer to a plate.

Add remaining 5 minced garlic cloves, along with prosciutto, to roasting pan and cook, stirring, until garlic is golden. Add wine and simmer to reduce by half, about a minute. Add tomatoes and enough water to make a saucelike consistency. Bring to a simmer, add meatballs, and cook, loosely covered with heavy-duty foil, to blend flavors, 10 to 15 minutes. Still on medium-high heat, add 6 cups water and remaining 1 teaspoon salt to pan and return to a simmer. Add penne, cover loosely with foil, and cook, stirring gently and frequently, until pasta is tender, about 15 minutes. Remove foil and continue to simmer until sauce is thickened to your liking. Serve, sprinkling each portion with feta cheese.

DRINK A medium-bodied red, such as Italian Barbera, Chianti, light Côtes du Rhône, or Pinot Noir

One-Pot Penne
with Spinach-Feta Balls

SERVES 6 TO 8

These highly seasoned spinach "meat" balls will appeal to both vegetarians and carnivores alike. Although the balls tend to fall apart when heated the second time, leftovers are still wonderful.

8 garlic cloves, peeled, 3 left whole, 5 minced

4 packages (10 ounces each) frozen chopped spinach, thawed and squeezed dry

½ stick (4 tablespoons) butter, melted

1 cup crumbled feta cheese (generous 4½ ounces), plus more for topping

½ cup finely grated Parmesan cheese

1½ cups dry bread crumbs

1 teaspoon dried oregano

1¾ teaspoons salt, divided

4 large eggs

6 tablespoons olive oil, divided

½ teaspoon crushed red pepper flakes

1 cup dry red wine

2 cans (28 ounces each) crushed tomatoes

1 pound penne pasta

Adjust oven rack to lower-middle position and heat oven to 350 degrees. Heat a small skillet over medium-high heat. Add 3 whole garlic cloves and toast until spotty brown, about 5 minutes. Remove garlic from skillet, smash, and mince.

Meanwhile, break up spinach into a medium bowl. With a fork, mix in butter, cheeses, bread crumbs, oregano, and ¾ teaspoon salt.

Mix eggs and minced toasted garlic together in a small bowl and stir into spinach mixture with fork until thoroughly combined. Using a 2-tablespoon measure, such as a coffee scoop, form mixture into about 36 balls.

Coat a large heavy roasting pan with 2 tablespoons oil. Add spinach balls and roast in oven until firm, about 20 minutes. Transfer to a plate and set aside.

Add remaining ¼ cup oil, pepper flakes, and remaining 5 minced garlic cloves to roasting pan and set over medium-high heat. Cook, stirring, until garlic is golden, a couple of minutes. Add wine and simmer to reduce by half, about a minute. Add tomatoes and enough water to make a saucelike consistency. Bring to a simmer, add spinach balls, reduce heat to medium-low, and cook, loosely covered with heavy-duty foil, to blend flavors, 10 to 15 minutes. Increase heat to medium-high, add 6 cups water and remaining 1 teaspoon salt, and return to a simmer. Add penne, cover loosely with foil, and cook, stirring gently and frequently, until pasta is tender, about 15 minutes. Remove foil and continue to simmer until sauce is thickened to your liking. Serve, sprinkling each portion with feta cheese.

APPETIZER # Warm Tapenade

MAKES ABOUT 1 QUART

Unlike classic tapenade, which is a black Mediterranean-olive paste, this one is a colorful mix of roasted olives, capers, cherry tomatoes, and garlic. Heating the tapenade melds the flavors. The chunky spread is great to have on hand for predinner nibbles. Serve with toasted baguette slices (see page 60) or crackers. For those who don't want bread, set out toothpicks for spearing.

The tapenade can be refrigerated for a month or more.

3 **cups olives: mix of pimento-stuffed green, pitted kalamatas, and canned ripe black, halved**

1 **pint cherry or grape tomatoes**

8 **garlic cloves, sliced**

½ **cup drained capers**

¼ **cup extra-virgin olive oil**

1 **tablespoon Italian seasoning**

Adjust oven rack to lower-middle position and heat oven to 425 degrees. Mix all ingredients on a large baking sheet. Roast until tapenade is fragrant and golden brown, 15 to 20 minutes. Serve warm or at room temperature.

> **INSTANT ALTERNATIVE:** Pick up a variety of olives—many grocery stores, in fact, have olive bars. Drain, mix, and drizzle with a little extra-virgin olive oil. Serve with a vase full of long, thin store-bought breadsticks and some thinly sliced prosciutto on a wooden cutting board.

Caesar Salad Flatbread Pizzas

SERVES 6 TO 8

These wonderfully crisp flatbreads act as both plate and crouton for this crowd-pleasing salad. The yeast-less dough can be made and rolled out before the oven is preheated. (If you don't have time to make the flatbreads, you can substitute a packaged 12-inch thin pizza crust.) If you're serving more than 6, increase the recipe by half.

½ **cup mayonnaise (light or regular)**

4 **large garlic cloves, minced**

¾ **teaspoon Worcestershire sauce**

FLATBREAD DOUGH

1 **cup bread or white whole-wheat flour, plus more for dusting**

½ **teaspoon salt**

1 **teaspoon extra-virgin olive oil**

1½ **tablespoons fresh lemon juice**

1½ **tablespoons extra-virgin olive oil**

6 **cups shredded hearts romaine lettuce**

Salt and freshly ground black pepper

6 **tablespoons finely grated Parmesan cheese, divided**

Adjust oven rack to lowest position and heat oven to 500 degrees (or 450 degrees for packaged pizza crust). Mix mayonnaise, garlic, and Worcestershire in a small bowl; set aside.

Flatbread Dough: Mix flour and salt in a food processor. Mix ⅓ cup warm water and oil together and pour over flour mixture; process to form a soft dough ball. If dough is too stiff (hard-clay texture), process in another teaspoon or so of water. Continue to process into a smooth but soft pliable dough, about 15 seconds. With floured hands, turn dough onto a lightly floured surface and cut into thirds. Working on one flatbread at a time, roll dough to an approximately 12-by-6-inch rectangle, coating with flour and turning as necessary to keep it from sticking. Transfer to a large (18-by-12-inch) baking sheet lined with parchment paper or a Silpat baking mat. Repeat with remaining dough to make 2 more flatbreads. Spread all but a generous 2 tablespoons mayonnaise mixture over flatbread dough or pizza crust and bake until heated through and crisp, 8 to 10 minutes.

Meanwhile, whisk lemon juice into remaining 2 tablespoons mayonnaise mixture. Drizzle olive oil over romaine in a medium bowl, along with a generous sprinkling of salt and pepper, and toss to coat. Add mayonnaise mixture and toss to coat. Add 4 tablespoons cheese; toss to coat again.

Top warm flatbreads with tossed salad. Sprinkle with remaining 2 tablespoons cheese. Serve immediately, halving each flatbread or cutting prepared pizza crust into 6 wedges.

SERVES 8

If you buy toasted hazelnuts instead of toasting the nuts yourself, you can assemble one of these cool sweet treats in just a couple of minutes. Or be creative and make up your own ice cream sandwich recipe, keeping in mind that the cookie should not be too thick, too hard, or too brittle. Sandwiches can be double wrapped and frozen for up to 1 week.

  1 cup chopped hazelnuts

 ⅓ cup chocolate-hazelnut spread (Nutella)

16 chocolate wafers, preferably Nabisco Famous

  1 pint premium chocolate ice cream

Heat oven to 350 degrees. Place nuts in a shallow baking pan large enough to hold them in a single layer; bake until fragrant and golden, 10 to 12 minutes. Cool to room temperature.

Meanwhile, smear a portion of hazelnut spread over one side of each wafer; set aside. Scoop 8 ice cream balls, a scant 3 tablespoons in size, and set on baking sheet in freezer until ready to assemble.

To assemble, set an ice cream ball on the hazelnut-spread side of each of 8 cookies; cap with remaining cookies, hazelnut-spread side down, and press to make a sandwich.

Roll sides of each ice cream sandwich in chopped hazelnuts and place in freezer until ready to serve.

> **INSTANT ALTERNATIVE:** Serve a premium ice cream confection from the grocery store, such as Dove Bars.

Quick, Creamy Lasagna

Chicken, Seafood, or Meatless Delicious: Spinach-Mushroom

When there's a crowd to feed, lasagna is the dish to serve. This recipe is irresistible, yet utterly simple. The surprise ingredient is the "white sauce," made by whisking together cream cheese, chicken broth, and basil.

The formula gives you three options—chicken, seafood, and spinach-mushroom—and the first two versions are especially quick.

APPETIZER Antipasti Flatbread Pizzas
Instant Alternative: Antipasti Naan "Pizzas"

SALAD Arugula with Roasted Peppers, White Beans, Red Onion, and Feta

DESSERT Amaretti Semifreddo with Chocolate and Toasted Almonds
Instant Alternative: Amaretti Ice Cream with Chocolate and Toasted Almonds

Quick, Creamy Lasagna

SERVES 8 TO 12

If using a prepared sauce, check the ingredient list—the shorter, the better. Avoid brands that contain sugar, or at least make sure sugar is last in the ingredient list. After it's baked, the lasagna will retain its heat for at least 30 minutes. Any leftover lasagna can be refrigerated for several days and reheated in the microwave. It can also be cut into individual portions and frozen. Assembled lasagnas can be frozen for a month or more; thaw before baking.

　　Salt
15　oven-ready (rippled-style, such as Ronzoni) lasagna noodles (from two 8-ounce boxes)
　4　cups chicken, seafood, or spinach-mushroom filling (recipes follow)
1½　teaspoons dried basil
12　ounces cream cheese, softened, divided
　½　cup chicken broth (vegetable broth for spinach-mushroom variation), divided
　1　jar (25–26 ounces) good marinara sauce (see headnote) or Simple Marinara (recipe follows)
　4　cups (1 pound) grated part-skim or whole-milk mozzarella cheese, divided
　¾　cup finely grated Parmesan cheese, divided

Adjust oven rack to lower-middle position and heat oven to 400 degrees. Dissolve 1½ tablespoons salt in 2 quarts piping hot tap water in a 13-by-9-inch baking dish. Add noodles and soak until soft, about 10 minutes. Drain in a colander.

Meanwhile, mix chicken, seafood, or spinach-mushroom filling with basil, 8 ounces cream cheese, and ¼ cup broth. Mix remaining 4 ounces cream cheese with remaining ¼ cup broth in a small bowl; set aside.

To assemble, smear ¼ cup marinara sauce over bottom of baking dish, then assemble 4 layers of each of the following: 3 lasagna noodles, a scant cup marinara, 1 cup filling mixture (for spinach-mushroom filling, use a scant cup), ¾ cup mozzarella, 2 tablespoons Parmesan. Top with remaining 3 noodles, cream cheese–broth mixture, remaining 1 cup mozzarella, and remaining ¼ cup Parmesan.

Spray one side of a large sheet of heavy-duty foil with vegetable-oil cooking spray. Cover baking dish with foil, oiled side down, and bake until bubbly throughout, 40 to 45 minutes. Leaving lasagna on same rack, turn oven to broil. Remove foil and broil until lasagna is spotty brown, 4 to 5 minutes. Remove from oven and let sit for 10 minutes. Cut into squares and serve.

Chicken

Shred 4 cups cooked chicken in a medium bowl.

Seafood

Mix 1 pound (2 cups) pasteurized lump crabmeat, patted dry, and 2 cups cooked salad shrimp in a medium bowl.

Spinach-Mushroom

Heat 2 tablespoons olive oil in a large (11- to 12-inch) deep skillet over medium-high heat. Add 1 pound sliced mushrooms, preferably baby bella, and cook, stirring, until tender and well browned, 5 to 7 minutes. Add 2 packages (10 ounces each) frozen chopped spinach, thawed and squeezed dry, and continue to cook, stirring and seasoning with salt and pepper to taste, until heated through. Transfer to a medium bowl.

Simple Marinara

MAKES A GENEROUS 3 CUPS

2 **tablespoons olive oil**

3 **garlic cloves, minced**

1 **can (28 ounces) crushed tomatoes, preferably fire-roasted**

Heat oil and garlic in a Dutch oven over medium-high heat. When garlic starts to sizzle, add tomatoes and enough water to make a sauce that is neither thin nor too thick. Bring to a simmer, reduce heat to medium-low, and continue to simmer, partially covered, to blend flavors, about 10 minutes.

DRINK **A full-bodied white, like Verdicchio or Orvieto Secco, or a light young red—Rioja or Chianti—or a rosé**

APPETIZER Antipasti Flatbread Pizzas

MAKES 8 SMALL FLATBREAD PIZZAS, SERVING 8 TO 10

*Baking salami, pepperoncini, and cheese on crisp flatbreads is a convenient, attractive way for guests to en-
joy antipasti. If serving these pizzas to an intergenerational crowd, be sure you make a few that are just plain
cheese—leave off the tapenade and pepperoncini, bake them naked, then top with cheese as instructed.
You can omit the salami or create whatever appetizer flatbread you like—just make sure you don't weigh
them down with too many ingredients. Olive tapenade is found in supermarkets; check in the gourmet aisle
or with the olives.*

FLATBREAD DOUGH

- **2 cups bread or white whole wheat flour, plus more for dusting**
- **1 teaspoon salt**
- **2 teaspoons extra-virgin olive oil**

- **1 cup olive tapenade (see headnote)**
- **2 cups (8 ounces) grated part-skim or whole-milk mozzarella cheese**
- **16 pepperoncini, stems removed and thinly sliced**
- **4 ounces very thin salami slices**

Adjust oven racks to lowest and upper-middle positions and heat oven to 500 degrees. Line each of two
large baking sheets with a Silpat baking mat or parchment paper.

Flatbread Dough: Mix flour and salt in a food processor. Mix ⅔ cup warm water and oil together and
pour over flour mixture; process to form soft clumps that easily come together. If dough is dry and sandy-
textured, process in another teaspoon or so of water. Continue to process into a smooth but soft pliable
dough, about 15 seconds. With floured hands, turn dough out onto a lightly floured surface and cut into
eighths; set 4 pieces aside.

Working with one dough piece at a time, roll each of 4 pieces into an approximately 12-by-4-inch rectangle, coating with flour and turning as necessary to keep it from sticking. Place rectangles crosswise on one
of the baking sheets and spread each with 2 tablespoons tapenade.

Bake on bottom oven rack until partially baked, dry, and golden, about 5 minutes. Remove from oven,
top each flatbread with ¼ cup cheese and a portion of pepperoncini, place on upper-middle rack, and continue to bake until crisp and spotty brown, about 5 minutes longer.

Meanwhile, prepare remaining 4 dough pieces, spreading with remaining tapenade and placing second
baking sheet on bottom oven rack when first sheet is transferred to upper-middle rack. When first sheet
comes out, top second batch of flatbreads with remaining cheese and remaining pepperoncini, and move
baking sheet to upper-middle rack. Top baked flatbread pizzas with salami rounds, folded in half to highlight
other pizza toppings. Cut each pizza into 6 to 8 pieces and serve.

INSTANT ALTERNATIVE: Because of their slightly irregular shape, store-bought naan breads (available in the grocery store's deli section or bread aisle) have a homemade pizza look. Place 4 store-bought naan (about 9 inches in diameter) on two large baking sheets. Using same quantities as in Antipasti Flatbread Pizzas, spread each naan with ¼ cup tapenade. Bake one sheet on lowest oven rack and the other on upper-middle rack in a 400-degree oven until partially baked, about 10 minutes. Remove from oven and top each naan with ½ cup cheese and a portion of pepperoncini. Return to oven, switching position of sheets, and continue to bake until naan bottoms are crisp and cheese has melted, about 5 minutes longer. Top with a portion of folded salami and serve. If you can't find naan, substitute two 12-inch thin pizza crusts, topping each with tapenade, 1 cup cheese, and some pepperoncini. Once pizzas are baked, top each with a portion of folded salami slices.

Arugula with Roasted Peppers, White Beans, Red Onion, and Feta

SERVES 8

The assertive ingredients in this salad—red onion, roasted peppers, and feta—partner well with the rich, creamy lasagna.

10	ounces (about 10 cups) prewashed baby arugula
½	medium red onion, thinly sliced
1 ½	cups thinly sliced strips roasted red peppers
	About 1½ cups canned white beans (from a 15- to 16-ounce can), drained
¾	cup crumbled feta cheese
6–8	tablespoons extra-virgin olive oil
	Salt and freshly ground black pepper
1–1½	tablespoons red wine vinegar

Place arugula, onion, peppers, beans, and feta in a large bowl. Just before serving, toss with 6 tablespoons olive oil and a generous sprinkling of salt and pepper. Taste, adding more oil, salt, or pepper, if necessary. Add 1 tablespoon vinegar and toss to coat, adding more, if necessary, to taste, and serve.

DESSERT # Amaretti Semifreddo with Chocolate and Toasted Almonds

SERVES 8

Folded-in whipped cream gives this ice cream a frozen-mousse consistency, while the liqueur-doused am-aretti cookies, toasted almonds, and bittersweet chocolate make for a delightful texture. Although the cookies gradually soften, leftover semifreddo is good for days if frozen in an airtight container. For optimal texture, however, the dessert should be prepared within a few hours of serving.

2½ ounces amaretti cookies (about 25 cookies), coarsely crushed (about 1¼ cups)

3 tablespoons almond liqueur, such as Disaronno, divided

¼ cup coarsely chopped salted or unsalted roasted almonds

2 ounces bittersweet chocolate, chopped into small chunks

½ cup heavy cream

1 pint premium vanilla ice cream, softened slightly (microwave on high power 15 to 30 seconds)

Place crushed cookies in a medium bowl. Drizzle 2 tablespoons almond liqueur over cookies; toss to coat. Add almonds and chocolate and toss to coat again. Whip cream and remaining 1 tablespoon almond liqueur with an electric mixer to stiff peaks in a medium bowl. Fold softened ice cream into cookie mixture until completely incorporated. Gently fold in whipped cream. Spoon into eight goblets and serve. Or cover and freeze until ready to serve.

> **INSTANT ALTERNATIVE:** Skip whipping and folding in cream.

Enchiladas

Spicy Chicken Enchiladas Verde with Sour Cream and Cilantro

Beef and Bean Enchiladas with Red Sauce

Creamy Seafood Enchiladas with Chiles and Green Olives

Say TGIF to friends and family with these quick-to-assemble enchiladas. You've got three options: chicken (made with shredded cooked chicken and spicy salsa verde), beef and bean (punched up with pepper Jack and creamy tomato sauce), and seafood (filled with cooked shrimp and crab tossed in a light piquant cream sauce). Heated in the microwave, leftover enchiladas make an easy lunch or dinner a day or two later.

APPETIZER The Best Seven-Layer Dip
Instant Alternative: Warm Jalapeño Cheese Dip

SALAD Mixed Greens with Jicama, Yellow Bell Pepper, and Red Onion

DESSERT Cinnamon Blondies
Instant Alternative: Brownie Bites with Coffee–Cream Cheese Frosting

Spicy Chicken Enchiladas Verde
with Sour Cream and Cilantro

SERVES 8

You can substitute a mixture of 1 pound lump crabmeat, picked over, and 8 ounces frozen cooked salad shrimp, thawed and drained, for the chicken here. The assembled enchiladas can be covered and refrigerated a day ahead.

- 4 **cups shredded cooked chicken**
- 4 **cups (32 ounces) store-bought salsa verde, divided**
- 8 **ounces grated Monterey Jack cheese (3 cups), divided**
- ½ **cup chopped fresh cilantro, divided**
- **Salt and freshly ground black pepper**
- 16 **corn tortillas**
- ½ **medium white onion, halved and thinly sliced**
- 1 **container (16 ounces) light sour cream**

Adjust oven rack to center position and heat oven to 400 degrees.

Mix chicken with ¾ cup salsa verde, 1½ cups cheese, ¼ cup cilantro, and salt and pepper to taste. Spread 1 cup salsa in a 13-by-9-inch baking dish.

Wrap tortillas in two damp paper towels and microwave on high power until warm and pliable, about 45 seconds. Spoon about ¼ cup chicken filling into a tortilla. Roll into a cylinder and place seam side down in baking dish. Repeat with remaining filling and tortillas. Drizzle enchiladas with 1½ cups salsa and sprinkle with remaining 1½ cups cheese. Spray a large sheet of heavy-duty foil with vegetable-oil cooking spray. Cover baking dish with foil, oiled side down, and bake until heated through, about 30 minutes. Remove foil, sprinkle with onion slices and remaining ¼ cup cilantro, let stand for a few minutes, and serve with sour cream and remaining 1¾ cup salsa verde.

DRINK **A full-bodied red, such as Petite Syrah**

Beef and Bean Enchiladas
with Red Sauce

SERVES 8

You can substitute 4 cups shredded cooked chicken or a mixture of 1 pound lump crabmeat, picked over, and 8 ounces frozen cooked salad shrimp, thawed and drained, for the beef and beans. The assembled enchiladas can be covered and refrigerated a day ahead.

1½	pounds lean ground beef
2	tablespoons chili powder
1	can (15.5 ounces) pinto beans, drained, half the beans mashed
8	ounces grated pepper Jack cheese (3 cups), divided
1	tablespoon olive oil
1	large white onion, halved, half finely diced, half thinly sliced
1	can (16 ounces) plus 1 can (8 ounces) tomato sauce
2	cups chicken broth
¼	cup sour cream, plus more for passing
16	corn tortillas

Adjust oven rack to center position and heat oven to 400 degrees.

Heat a large (11- to 12-inch) deep skillet over medium-high heat. Add ground beef and cook, stirring frequently, until meat loses its raw color and liquid evaporates, about 7 minutes. Add chili powder and continue to cook, stirring, until fragrant, about 2 minutes longer. Transfer to a medium bowl. Stir in mashed and whole beans, along with 1½ cups cheese.

Meanwhile, return unwashed skillet to burner and heat oil over medium-high. Add diced onion and cook, stirring frequently, until soft, 4 to 5 minutes. Add tomato sauce and simmer to tomato-paste consistency, stirring frequently and reducing heat if sputtering dramatically, 8 to 10 minutes. Add broth and bring to a simmer. Remove from heat and whisk in sour cream. Stir ¾ cup sauce into meat mixture and spread 1 cup sauce over bottom of a 13-by-9-inch baking dish.

Wrap tortillas in two damp paper towels and microwave on high power until warm and pliable, about 45 seconds. Spoon about ¼ cup meat mixture into a tortilla. Roll into a cylinder and place seam side down in baking dish. Repeat with remaining filling and tortillas. Drizzle enchiladas with 1½ cups sauce and sprinkle with remaining 1½ cups cheese. Spray a large sheet of heavy-duty foil with vegetable-oil cooking spray. Cover baking dish with foil, oiled side down, and bake until heated through, about 30 minutes. Remove foil and sprinkle with onion slices. Let stand for a few minutes and serve with sour cream and remaining sauce.

DRINK   **A spicy red, such as Zinfandel**

Creamy Seafood Enchiladas
with Chiles and Green Olives

SERVES 8

If you have a little more time, you can substitute cooked wild shrimp, cut into small bite-size pieces, for the salad shrimp. The assembled enchiladas can be covered and refrigerated a day ahead.

- 1 pound pasteurized lump crabmeat, picked over
- 8 ounces frozen cooked salad shrimp, thawed and drained
- ¾ cup coarsely chopped pimento-stuffed olives
- 8 ounces grated Monterey Jack cheese (3 cups), divided
- 2 bottles (8 ounces each) clam juice
- 1 can (12 ounces) evaporated milk
- 4 garlic cloves, minced
- 3 tablespoons butter
- ⅓ cup all-purpose flour
- ½ cup finely grated Parmesan cheese
- 1 can (4.5 ounces) chopped green chiles, undrained
- 16 corn tortillas

Mix crab, shrimp, olives, and 1½ cups Monterey Jack cheese in a medium bowl.

Microwave clam juice, evaporated milk, and garlic in a 2-quart microwave-safe bowl on high until steamy hot, 6 to 8 minutes.

Meanwhile, heat butter in a large saucepan over medium heat. When foaming subsides, whisk in flour until well blended. Pour in hot milk mixture all at once and whisk vigorously until sauce is smooth and starts to thicken. Whisk in Parmesan and chiles and continue to simmer until sauce is cream-soup consistency.

Stir ¾ cup sauce into filling and spread 1 cup sauce over bottom of a 13-by-9-inch baking dish.

Wrap tortillas in two damp paper towels and microwave on high power until warm and pliable, about 45 seconds. Spoon about ¼ cup seafood filling into a tortilla. Roll into a cylinder and place seam side down in baking dish. Repeat with remaining filling and tortillas. Drizzle enchiladas with 1 cup sauce and sprinkle with remaining 1½ cups Monterey Jack. Spray a large sheet of heavy-duty foil with vegetable-oil cooking spray. Cover baking dish with foil, oiled side down, and bake until heated through, about 30 minutes. Uncover and let stand for a few minutes. Warm remaining sauce (thin with water, if necessary, to cream-soup consistency) and serve with enchiladas.

DRINK **A full-bodied white, such as Chardonnay or Torrontes from Argentina**

APPETIZER The Best Seven-Layer Dip

SERVES UP TO 12

The refried beans in this classic dip are perked up and softened with green chiles, a squirt of lime juice, and a little spice. Mixing mayonnaise into the sour cream lightens a normally heavy layer, and draining off some of the salsa's juice keeps things neat. If you can't find ripe avocados, use 16 ounces (about 1½ cups) prepared guacamole and freshen it up by seasoning it generously with fresh lime juice. Except for sprinkling on the scallions, the dip can be covered and refrigerated for up to 2 days.

1   **can (16 ounces) refried beans (traditional variety)**

1   **can (4.5 ounces) chopped green chiles, undrained**

3   **tablespoons fresh lime juice, divided**

2   **teaspoons chili powder**

¼   **teaspoon ground cumin**

    Salt

3   **ripe avocados, halved, pitted, and flesh spooned out**

1   **cup sour cream (light or regular)**

½   **cup mayonnaise**

1   **jar (16 ounces) salsa, drained to equal 1 cup, juices discarded**

¾   **cup sliced canned black olives, drained**

1   **cup (about 4 ounces) grated pepper Jack cheese**

½   **cup thinly sliced scallion greens**

    Taste-Like-Fried Tortillas (page 154) or one 14- to 16-ounce bag store-bought tortilla chips

Mix beans, chiles, 1 tablespoon lime juice, chili powder, cumin, and a pinch of salt in a small bowl. In a separate bowl, mash avocados with a fork and stir in remaining 2 tablespoons lime juice and ½ teaspoon salt. Mix sour cream and mayonnaise in a separate small bowl. Spread bean mixture, then avocados, then sour cream mixture, and, finally, salsa in a 9-inch deep-dish pie plate or similar-size pan. Sprinkle with olives, then cheese. Just before serving, sprinkle with scallions. Serve with tortillas or tortilla chips for dipping.

INSTANT ALTERNATIVE: Make Warm Jalapeño Cheese Dip. Microwave 1 can (12 ounces) evaporated milk in a 1-quart Pyrex measuring cup until steamy. Meanwhile, heat 2 tablespoons butter in a large saucepan over medium heat. Whisk in 3 tablespoons all-purpose flour and ½ teaspoon turmeric and, finally, the hot milk until creamy and thick. Whisk in 8 ounces grated pepper Jack cheese (2 cups) until melted and smooth. Stir in 1 cup prepared salsa, heat through, and serve.

Mixed Greens with Jicama, Yellow Bell Pepper, and Red Onion

SERVES 8

This salad's crisp vegetables and cool creamy dressing balance the contrasting texture and flavor of the soft, spicy enchiladas. Much like a water chestnut, jicama contributes clean flavor and a snappy texture to the salad.

- **10 ounces (about 15 cups) prewashed mixed baby greens**
- **½ medium jicama, peeled and cut into short strips**
- **1 small red or yellow bell pepper, cut into short strips**
- **½ medium red onion, thinly sliced**
- **½ cup Simple Creamy Dressing (recipe below) or to taste**

Place greens, jicama, bell pepper, and red onion in a large bowl. Just before serving, toss salad with dressing.

Simple Creamy Dressing

MAKES 1½ CUPS

The dressing can be refrigerated in an airtight container for up to 3 weeks.

- **⅓ cup light mayonnaise**
- **⅓ cup light sour cream**
- **⅔ cup buttermilk**
- **2 tablespoons rice wine vinegar**
- **¼ teaspoon garlic powder**
- **¼ teaspoon each salt and freshly ground black pepper**

In a small bowl, whisk mayonnaise, sour cream, buttermilk, vinegar, garlic powder, and salt and pepper together.

Cinnamon Blondies

MAKES 25 SMALL BARS

Here's one of the simplest, quickest bars you can make. If you like, vary them by stirring extras into the finished batter, choosing from two of the three optional stir-ins.

For a 13-by-9-inch pan of blondies, simply double the ingredients and increase the baking time to 45 minutes.

- 1½ cups cake flour
- 1½ teaspoons baking powder
- 2 teaspoons ground cinnamon
- ¼ teaspoon salt
- 1½ cups packed light brown sugar
- 1½ sticks (12 tablespoons) unsalted butter, melted
- 2 large eggs
- 1½ teaspoons vanilla extract

OPTIONAL STIR-INS
- ¾ cup dried cranberries, dried cherries, raisins, or coarsely chopped dried apricots or dates
- ¾ cup coarsely chopped pecans, walnuts, slivered almonds, pistachios, hazelnuts, or macadamia nuts
- ¾ cup chocolate chips or coarsely chopped white, semisweet, or bittersweet chocolate chunks

Adjust oven rack to lowest position and heat oven to 325 degrees. Spray an 8-inch square metal baking pan with vegetable-oil cooking spray. Fold a 16-inch length of heavy-duty foil to 7½ inches wide and lay it across pan bottom and up two sides so you have foil overhangs to pull blondies from pan. Spray foil with vegetable-oil cooking spray.

Whisk flour, baking powder, cinnamon, and salt in a medium bowl. Whisk brown sugar into butter in a medium bowl. Whisk eggs and vanilla together in a small bowl, then whisk into butter mixture. Whisk in dry ingredients until just combined. Fold in 2 optional stir-ins, if using. Pour batter into prepared pan. Bake until blondies are just set, about 40 minutes. Remove from oven and let cool for 5 minutes. Using foil handles, pull blondies from pan, set on a wire rack, and cool to room temperature. Cut into squares and serve.

INSTANT ALTERNATIVE: Serve Brownie Bites with Coffee–Cream Cheese Frosting. Make frosting by beating 6 ounces softened cream cheese and 3 tablespoons softened unsalted butter with 6 tablespoons confectioners' sugar and 1½ teaspoons instant espresso or coffee powder. Smear frosting on top of 12 store-bought brownie bites (located in the grocery store's bakery section or cookie aisle). Garnish with chocolate-covered coffee beans or an ounce or so of grated bittersweet chocolate.

Tamale Pie

Thick chili meets moist cornbread. A great party dish, this is lightened up by using ground turkey instead of the usual beef.

APPETIZER Taste-Like-Fried Tortillas with Lighter Guacamole
Instant Alternative: Tortilla Chips with Simplest Guacamole

SALAD Confetti Slaw with Jicama, Bell Pepper, and Scallions

DESSERT Pineapple Upside-Down Biscuits
Instant Alternative: Simpler Pineapple Upside-Down Biscuits

Tamale Pie

SERVES 6

You can use ground beef or even meat-loaf mix in place of the turkey. Onion lovers, sprinkle the casserole with ½ thinly sliced red onion along with the cheese and cilantro. You can make the tamale pie a day ahead, including topping it with the cornmeal mush. Place a sheet of plastic wrap directly on the pie to prevent a skin from forming. An hour or so before serving, adjust the oven rack to the lower-middle position and heat the oven to 400 degrees. Remove the plastic wrap, top the pie with cheese, cover with heavy-duty foil, and bake until heated through, about 30 minutes. Remove the foil, sprinkle with the cilantro and the red onion, if you like, and then follow the broiling and resting instructions in the recipe.

Any leftovers can be covered and refrigerated for up to 3 days and reheated in the microwave.

1½ **pounds ground turkey (94% lean)**

    Salt

2 **tablespoons plus 2 teaspoons chili powder, divided**

1½ **cans (about 16 ounces) pinto beans, undrained, ½ can mashed**

1 **can (4.5 ounces) chopped green chiles, undrained**

2 **cans (2.25 ounces each) sliced black olives, drained**

1 **jar (16 ounces) store-bought salsa (2 cups)**

½ **cup chopped fresh cilantro, divided**

1 **cup cornmeal**

1 **cup (8 ounces) grated sharp cheddar cheese**

Adjust oven rack to middle position and turn on broiler. Heat a large (11- to 12-inch) deep skillet with an ovenproof handle over medium-high heat. Add ground turkey and cook, stirring frequently and seasoning lightly with salt, until it loses its raw color, a couple of minutes. Stir in 2 tablespoons chili powder, then beans, chiles, olives, salsa, and ¼ cup cilantro and simmer to blend flavors, about 5 minutes.

Meanwhile, bring 3 cups water, cornmeal, remaining 2 teaspoons chili powder, and 1 teaspoon salt to a boil in a medium saucepan, whisking frequently, until mixture thickens to mush. Pour cornmeal mush over hot meat mixture, spreading with a spatula to completely cover. Sprinkle with cheese and remaining ¼ cup cilantro. Broil until cheese melts and mush gets a little crusty, about 5 minutes. Let rest for 5 minutes before serving.

DRINK   **A dry rosé or beer**

APPETIZER # Taste-Like-Fried Tortillas with Lighter Guacamole

MAKES A SCANT 2 CUPS

By substituting less expensive, lower-calorie green peas and water for some of the avocados (a trick I learned at Rancho La Puerta Fitness Resort and Spa, in Baja California), you're saving calories and bucks—and no one will ever suspect.

The chips are brushed with a minimal amount of oil, so even though they're baked, they actually taste fried. The guacamole can be covered with plastic wrap placed directly over the surface and refrigerated for up to 4 hours. If you don't have time to make the tortillas, simply serve the guacamole with a 14- to 16-ounce bag of store-bought tortilla chips.

6	corn tortillas (from an 11-ounce package)
1½	tablespoons olive oil
	Kosher salt
¾	cup frozen green peas, thawed
3	ripe Hass avocados, pitted, peeled, and coarsely smashed
3	scallions, thinly sliced
3	tablespoons chopped fresh cilantro
1½	tablespoons fresh lime juice
½	teaspoon garlic powder
½	teaspoon hot red pepper sauce
¾	teaspoon salt

Adjust oven racks to upper- and lower-middle positions and heat oven to 400 degrees. Arrange tortillas in a single layer on a cookie sheet. Brush both sides of each tortilla with oil and generously sprinkle with kosher salt. Bake until crisp and golden brown, about 12 minutes.

Meanwhile, place peas and 3 tablespoons water in a blender and process until smooth, about 30 seconds. Transfer to a medium bowl. Stir in remaining ingredients. Serve with tortillas.

> **INSTANT ALTERNATIVE:** Make Simplest Guacamole by mashing 3 small Hass avocados with a fork until chunky; stir in salt and fresh lime juice to taste. If you can't find ripe avocados, purchase store-bought guacamole and freshen it with a few squirts of fresh lime juice, a sprinkling of salt, and chopped fresh cilantro to taste. Serve with Taste-Like-Fried Tortillas (above) or a 14- to 16-ounce bag of store-bought tortilla chips.

SALAD Confetti Slaw with Jicama, Bell Pepper, and Scallions

SERVES 6

Crisp slaw is the perfect foil for this soft cornmeal-topped chili casserole. For a more festive slaw, use a blend of purple and green cabbage. The dressing and salad can be covered and refrigerated separately for several hours before serving.

3 tablespoons frozen orange juice concentrate, thawed

3 tablespoons rice wine vinegar

3 tablespoons extra-virgin olive oil

1 pound shredded purple cabbage (packaged variety is fine)

½ small jicama, peeled and cut into thin bite-size strips

½ small red bell pepper, cut into thin bite-size strips

3 small scallions, thinly sliced

¼ cup chopped fresh cilantro

Place orange juice concentrate, vinegar, and olive oil in a 1-cup measuring cup and whisk to combine. Mix remaining ingredients in a large bowl. Pour dressing over slaw, toss, and serve.

DESSERT Pineapple Upside-Down Biscuits

SERVES UP TO 10

Much quicker to assemble and bake than an upside-down cake, these biscuits are just as irresistible. A group of guests smaller than ten will make fast work of the remains (and, if not, there's always breakfast!). Up to the point of adding the buttermilk, the biscuit mixture can be prepared up to a week ahead and frozen. A couple of hours before serving, assemble the dessert and refrigerate until ready to bake. Serve with a scoop of premium vanilla or butter pecan ice cream, if you like.

PINEAPPLE
- ¾ **cup packed dark brown sugar**
- 3 **tablespoons unsalted butter**
- 1½ **cups chopped fresh pineapple**

BISCUITS
- 2 **cups bleached all-purpose flour**
- 2 **teaspoons baking powder**
- ¼ **teaspoon baking soda**
- 1 **teaspoon sugar**
- ¾ **teaspoon salt**
- ¾ **stick (6 tablespoons) unsalted butter, frozen**
- 1 **cup cold buttermilk, plus a few extra teaspoons if necessary**

Adjust oven rack to middle position and heat oven to 450 degrees.

Pineapple: Heat brown sugar and butter in a small saucepan over medium heat to a spreadable consistency. Pour into a 9-inch round cake pan, tilting to coat pan bottom; top with pineapple.

Biscuits: Mix flour, baking powder, baking soda, sugar, and salt with a fork in a medium bowl. Using a box grater, coarsely grate frozen butter into dry ingredients, mixing quickly with fingertips to evenly blend. Stir in buttermilk with a fork, adding extra droplets of buttermilk over any dry patches, if necessary, and mix until dough just comes together.

Turn dough onto a floured surface. With your fingers, pinch dough into 10 rough rounds and arrange over pineapple. Bake until biscuits are golden brown and pineapple topping is bubbly, about 20 minutes. Invert onto a serving plate and serve immediately.

INSTANT ALTERNATIVE: Make Simpler Pineapple Upside-Down Biscuits. Adjust oven rack to lowest position and heat oven to 450 degrees. Heat ¾ cup packed dark brown sugar and 3 tablespoons unsalted butter in a small saucepan over medium heat until melted. Pour into a 9-inch round cake pan, tilting to completely coat pan bottom. Top with 1½ cups chopped fresh pineapple. Arrange 10 refrigerated dinner rolls from an 11.3-ounce can (my preference) or 10 small (not Grands) flaky biscuits from a 12-ounce can over pineapple. Bake until rolls or biscuits are well browned and pineapple topping is bubbling throughout, about 18 minutes. Invert onto a plate and serve warm with a scoop of premium vanilla or butter pecan ice cream. (If making this dessert from start to finish at one time, heat butter and sugar in cake pan in preheating oven.)

Chicken Biryani American-Style

Distinctly spicy (but not too), biryani (bir-ee-*ah*-nee) is a wonderfully aromatic Indian chicken and rice dish.

APPETIZER Indian Scotch Eggs
Instant Alternative: Pappadams and Major Grey Chutney with Cilantro and Dried Cranberries

SALAD Baby Spinach with Mango, Red Onion, and Cilantro

DESSERT Apricot-Date-Pistachio Bars
Instant Alternative: Sweet Cream Croissants with Pistachios and Dried Apricots

Chicken Biryani American-Style

SERVES 6

Except for the final assembly and 30-minute bake, this dish can be made 2 hours ahead. Using boneless, skinless chicken thighs rather than breasts makes the dish moist and meaty, but you can substitute boneless, skinless chicken breasts if you prefer. Hope for leftovers—heated up the next day, biryani is almost as good as the first time around. The recipe easily doubles; just use a roasting pan set over two burners.

2	pounds (about 8 medium) boneless, skinless chicken thighs, cut into 1- to 1½-inch chunks
	Salt and freshly ground black pepper
3	tablespoons butter, divided
1	large onion, chopped, divided
1½	tablespoons minced or grated fresh gingerroot
½	teaspoon crushed red pepper flakes
2	tablespoons garam masala (found in the grocery store's spice or international aisle)
¾	cup plain low-fat yogurt
1½	tablespoons fresh lime juice
1½	cups basmati rice
½	teaspoon saffron threads
1	cup light coconut milk
2	cups chicken broth, divided
½	cup dark raisins
¼	cup coarsely chopped roasted cashews
¼	cup chopped fresh cilantro

Generously sprinkle chicken with salt and pepper; set aside. Heat 2 tablespoons butter in a large (11- to 12-inch) deep ovenproof skillet over medium heat. Add half of onion, ginger, and pepper flakes and cook, stirring, until tender, 4 to 5 minutes. Add garam masala and continue to cook until fragrant, 1 to 2 minutes longer. Add chicken and, stirring constantly, cook until it loses its raw color, about 5 minutes. Add yogurt and lime juice and cook, stirring to loosen brown bits, until juices thicken slightly, 2 to 3 minutes longer. Transfer chicken mixture to a bowl. Wipe out pan with a paper towel; return pan to medium heat.

Melt remaining 1 tablespoon butter, add remaining onion, and cook, stirring, until soft, 4 to 5 minutes. Stir in rice and saffron. Stir in coconut milk, 1 cup broth, raisins, and ½ teaspoon salt. Cover with heavy-duty foil, bring to a simmer, and cook undisturbed until liquid is absorbed, about 15 minutes. (Chicken and rice can be covered and set aside separately at room temperature for up to 2 hours.)

About 45 minutes before serving, adjust oven rack to lower-middle position and heat oven to 375 degrees. Scoop about one third of the rice into a medium bowl. Spread remaining rice evenly over bottom of skillet. Pour chicken and juices over rice in skillet, then top with remaining rice. Pour remaining 1 cup broth over rice and cover pan with foil. Bake until heated through and rice starts to crust around the edges, about 30 minutes. Remove from oven, sprinkle with cashews and cilantro, and serve.

DRINK A full-bodied red such as Côtes du Rhône (a Châteauneuf-du-Pape or Gigondas, if the budget allows), a fruity white such as Gewürztraminer, Pinot Gris, or Riesling, or a flavorful pale ale

Indian Scotch Eggs

MAKES 4 DOZEN WEDGES

Boiled eggs enrobed in ground sausage and baked, these little cocktail nibbles are a major hit whenever they're served. Here, lighter turkey sausage takes the place of the traditional pork, and a smidgen of garam masala or curry powder will keep people guessing about that elusive flavor. Leftovers are great for breakfast or in a lunch salad . . . or with a glass of wine tomorrow night.

If you can find only sausage links, simply remove the ground meat from its casing.

1	pound bulk (not cooked) Italian turkey sausage (see headnote)
2	tablespoons chopped fresh cilantro
2	teaspoons garam masala or curry powder
6	large boiled eggs (see headnote on page 180), peeled
½	cup plain dry bread crumbs
	Major Grey Chutney with Cilantro and Dried Cranberries (optional)

Adjust oven rack to lower-middle position and heat oven to 350 degrees. Using a fork, mix sausage with cilantro and garam masala. Divide sausage into 6 equal portions. Working on one portion at a time, press sausage mixture into a patty. Set 1 egg on patty and work sausage around it to completely enclose. Coat with bread crumbs and place on a baking sheet. Repeat with remaining sausage, eggs, and bread crumbs. Lightly spray eggs with vegetable-oil cooking spray. Bake, turning every 10 to 15 minutes, until golden brown, about 45 minutes. When eggs are ready, cool for 5 minutes. Cut each egg into quarters, then halve each quarter, and top with chutney garnish, if desired.

Major Grey Chutney with Cilantro and Dried Cranberries (optional)

2	tablespoons or ½ cup Major Grey Chutney
1½	teaspoons or 2 tablespoons coarsely chopped dried cranberries
1	teaspoon or 4 teaspoons minced fresh cilantro
½	teaspoon or 2 teaspoons rice wine vinegar

In a small bowl, mix chutney ingredients together, using the smaller quantities. Use larger quantities if serving with pappadams.

INSTANT ALTERNATIVE: Serve a stack of pappadams—thin, crisp lentil crackers. Unless you can find them in the grocery store's snack aisle, pappadams are more often found in the international section and must be cooked before serving, but it's a quick process. Lightly brush each pappadam with vegetable or canola oil (about 1 tablespoon for 12 pappadams). Microwave them one at a time (about 45 seconds on high power) or bake them, 6 at a time, on a baking sheet set on the lower-middle rack of a 400-degree oven until light golden brown, about 3 minutes (they crisp as they cool). Serve with Major Grey Chutney with Cilantro and Dried Cranberries, using the larger quantities.

SALAD Baby Spinach with Mango, Red Onion, and Cilantro

SERVES 6

Spinach and mango salad is a soothing contrast to the spicy chicken and rice.
Instead of the dressing here, you can substitute 1 cup Orange Vinaigrette (page 18), if you like.

7	ounces (about 10 cups) prewashed baby spinach
1	large mango or 2 small, peeled, pitted, and diced
¼	medium red onion, thinly sliced
2	tablespoons chopped fresh cilantro
4–6	tablespoons extra-virgin olive oil
	Salt and freshly ground black pepper
1½–2	tablespoons rice wine vinegar

Place spinach, mango, onion, and cilantro in a large bowl. Just before serving, toss with 4 tablespoons olive oil and a generous sprinkling of salt and pepper. Taste, adding more oil, salt, or pepper, if necessary. Add 1½ tablespoons vinegar and toss to coat, adding more, if necessary, to taste, and serve.

Apricot-Date-Pistachio Bars

MAKES 16 BARS

Chock-full of nuts, dried fruit, and coconut, these bars are rich and satisfying. If you want to make them ahead, the uncut bars can be double wrapped and frozen for a month. The cut bars can be stored in an airtight tin for up to a week. If you omit the cardamom, there's no need to heat the evaporated milk.

½ cup bleached all-purpose flour

½ cup old-fashioned oatmeal

6 tablespoons packed light brown sugar

½ stick (4 tablespoons) unsalted butter, melted

¾ cup sweetened condensed milk

½ teaspoon ground cardamom (optional; see headnote)

1 cup sweetened flaked coconut

1 cup shelled roasted pistachios

1 cup chopped pitted dates

1 cup chopped dried apricots

Adjust oven rack to lower-middle position and heat oven to 325 degrees. Spray an 8-inch square metal baking pan with vegetable-oil cooking spray. Fold a 16-inch length of heavy-duty foil to 7½ inches wide and lay it across pan bottom and up two sides so you have foil overhangs to remove bars from pan. Spray foil with vegetable-oil cooking spray.

Mix flour, oatmeal, and sugar in a medium bowl. Stir in butter with a fork until well mixed and clumps form. Spread ¾ cup oatmeal mixture into pan, pressing to form a thin crust on bottom.

Meanwhile, heat condensed milk and cardamom to a simmer in a small saucepan over low heat to blend flavors. Mix coconut, pistachios, dates, and apricots in a medium bowl. Add milk mixture and stir to combine. Pour over oatmeal mixture in pan, using a rubber spatula to press mixture in place. Sprinkle remaining oatmeal mixture over filling.

Bake until lightly golden, about 30 minutes. Set on a wire rack and cool for 5 minutes. Using foil handles, remove bars from pan and cool to room temperature. Cut into squares and serve.

INSTANT ALTERNATIVE: Serve Sweet Cream Croissants with Pistachios and Dried Apricots. Split 6 small (or 3 large) good-quality flaky croissants in half lengthwise, replace tops, and heat on lower-middle rack of a 325-degree oven until crisp and warm, about 10 minutes. Remove from oven and place on a large platter. Remove croissant tops and drizzle bottoms with half of ⅓ cup warm sweetened condensed milk. Cap croissants, drizzle with remaining condensed milk, and sprinkle with ¼ cup each chopped pistachios and finely diced dried apricots. Halve large croissants crosswise and serve. (Serves 6)

Shells and Cheese for Everyone

This mac and cheese is friendly enough for the kids but has real adult appeal too—it's super-creamy and moist.

My daughter, who's extremely picky about macaroni and cheese (and doesn't like cottage cheese), loves this recipe.

APPETIZER Pulled Barbecue Chicken Sliders
Instant Alternative: Pulled Barbecue Chicken or Pork Sliders

SALAD PLT Salad

DESSERT Chocolate Rice Krispies Treats

Shells and Cheese for Everyone

SERVES 8 TO 12

Cheddar, Parmesan, sour cream, and cottage cheese keep this macaroni and cheese invitingly moist and gooey. Even if you're not a fan of cottage cheese, don't skip over this recipe: the cottage cheese does its work unnoticed. Up to the point of adding the bread crumbs, the macaroni and cheese can be covered and refrigerated a day in advance. Return to room temperature (microwave for speedy results) before topping and baking. Leftovers heat well—just add a little water, cover, and microwave until hot.

> **Salt**
> 1 **pound medium-size pasta shells**
> 1 **pound grated sharp cheddar cheese**
> 1 **container (16 ounces) cottage cheese**
> ½ **cup finely grated Parmesan cheese**
> 1 **container (16 ounces) light or regular sour cream**
> **Freshly ground black pepper**
> 1 **cup plain dry bread crumbs**
> 3 **tablespoons chopped fresh parsley**
> 3 **tablespoons butter, melted**

Adjust oven rack to lower-middle position and heat oven to 350 degrees. Coat a 13-by-9-inch baking dish with vegetable-oil cooking spray.

Bring 2 quarts water and 1 tablespoon salt to a boil in a large soup kettle over high heat. Using package directions as a guide and stirring frequently at first to keep it from sticking, boil pasta, partially covered, until just tender. Drain.

Meanwhile, mix cheeses and sour cream in a large bowl. Add hot pasta and toss to coat. Adjust seasonings, including salt and pepper to taste. Transfer to baking dish.

Mix bread crumbs, parsley, and butter in a small bowl and sprinkle evenly over shells and cheese. Bake until casserole is bubbly and crumbs are golden brown, 30 to 35 minutes. Serve.

DRINK **Any fruity young red, such as Beaujolais**

APPETIZER Pulled Barbecue Chicken Sliders

MAKES 2 DOZEN

Who can resist a mound of barbecue chicken nestled in a warm, soft party roll with a little dill pickle chip to balance the sweet sauce? Using rotisserie chicken and a good-quality prepared barbecue sauce, these substantial little nibbles come together very quickly. Covered with plastic wrap to prevent the rolls from drying out, the sliders can be assembled a couple of hours ahead. Pop into the oven close to serving.

1 **package (24) small party rolls**
2 **cups shredded rotisserie or other cooked chicken**
¾ **cup your favorite barbecue sauce (mine is Cattlemen's)**
24 **dill pickle slices**

Adjust oven rack to lower-middle position and heat oven to 350 degrees. Break rolls into individual buns and split in half horizontally. Mix chicken and barbecue sauce in a medium bowl. Top each roll bottom with a heaping tablespoon of pulled chicken and a pickle slice and cap each with roll top. Place rolls on a baking sheet and bake until warmed through, about 8 minutes. Serve.

> **INSTANT ALTERNATIVE:** Make the same mini sandwiches using 1 container (18 ounces or a scant 2 cups) store-bought refrigerated pulled chicken or pork in place of the cooked chicken and barbecue sauce.

 **PLT Salad**

Acidic tomatoes balance the creaminess of the macaroni and cheese, and crisp prosciutto bits add a crunchy flair. If you like, use the frying oil, which adds a meaty complexity to the salad, as part of the dressing.

½ cup extra-virgin olive oil, divided (or see headnote)

8 thin slices (about 4 ounces) prosciutto, sliced crosswise into narrow strips and separated

10 ounces (about 15 cups) prewashed mixed baby greens

2 heaping cups grape tomatoes, halved and lightly salted

Salt and freshly ground black pepper

1½–2 tablespoons fresh lemon juice

Heat ¼ cup olive oil in a large skillet over medium heat. Add prosciutto and fry, stirring frequently, until frizzled and slightly darker in color, 4 to 5 minutes. Drain on paper towels. Pour olive oil from pan into a measuring cup and add more oil, if necessary, to equal 6 tablespoons.

Place greens, tomatoes, and prosciutto in a large bowl. Just before serving, toss with the 6 tablespoons olive oil and a generous sprinkling of salt and pepper. Taste, adding up to 2 more tablespoons oil and additional salt or pepper, if necessary. Add 1½ tablespoons lemon juice and toss to coat, adding more, if necessary, to taste, and serve.

Chocolate Rice Krispies Treats

MAKES 16 SQUARES

All the fun of a regular Rice Krispies treat—and chocolate too! If it's kids you're trying to please, use mini chocolate chips. For those with more sophisticated tastes, substitute an equal amount of chopped high-quality bittersweet chocolate. Wrapped in foil (the foil overhang from the pan works well) and plastic wrap, these bars can be made a day ahead. It doesn't get any simpler.

- ½ stick (4 tablespoons) unsalted butter
- ¼ cup unsweetened cocoa powder
- 1 jar (7 ounces) marshmallow cream
- 5 cups Rice Krispies
- ⅔ cup semisweet chocolate mini morsels, divided

Spray an 8-inch square metal baking pan with vegetable-oil cooking spray. Fold a 16-inch length of heavy-duty foil to 7½ inches wide and lay it across pan bottom and up the sides so you have foil overhangs to pull bars from pan. Spray foil with vegetable-oil cooking spray.

Heat butter in a small saucepan over medium-low heat. Stir in cocoa powder until mixture starts to bubble. Remove from heat and stir in marshmallow cream. Return to heat and continue to cook, stirring, until marshmallow cream has melted and mixture is smooth. Remove from heat and stir in Rice Krispies and ⅓ cup chocolate chips. Using a rubber spatula, press mixture into prepared pan. Sprinkle with remaining ⅓ cup chocolate chips, pressing them into Rice Krispies mixture so they adhere. Let stand until cool, about 15 minutes. Using foil overhangs, pull bar from pan. Cut into 16 squares and serve.

Roasting Pan Complete

Roast Salmon

WITH POTATOES, ASPARAGUS, AND LEMON-DILL-CAPER DRIZZLE

Still-life beautiful, this platter of roast salmon, asparagus, and new potatoes is perfect for a simple, elegant spring lunch or dinner.

APPETIZER Shrimp Wonton Crisps with Asian Pesto
Instant Alternative: Crispy Egg Roll Bites with Duck Sauce

SALAD Deviled Eggs on Butter Lettuce with Honey-Mustard Dressing

DESSERT Meringue Pastries with Strawberry Sauce
Instant Alternative: Strawberry Cream Parfaits with Coconut Macaroon Crumble

Roast Salmon with Potatoes, Asparagus, and Lemon-Dill-Caper Drizzle

SERVES 6

Here's a clever way to use your oven to the fullest. Set the baking sheet of potatoes on the bottom rack and the salmon on the upper-middle rack in a cold oven and then turn it on. Cooked in the preheating oven, the potatoes brown beautifully as the salmon roasts. Slide the cooked salmon onto a serving platter, and cook the asparagus on the same baking sheet while the fish rests. Arrange the potatoes and asparagus around the salmon.

1	whole side salmon (2½–3 pounds)
5	tablespoons olive oil, divided
	Salt and freshly ground black pepper
2	pounds fingerling potatoes or small red new potatoes, halved
2	bunches (2 pounds) asparagus, tough ends snapped off
¼	cup coarsely chopped fresh parsley
¼	cup coarsely chopped fresh dill leaves, plus dill sprigs for garnish
¼	cup capers plus 2 teaspoons caper juice
3	medium scallions, thinly sliced
1½	teaspoons finely grated lemon zest, plus lemon slices for garnish
6	tablespoons extra-virgin olive oil

Set salmon on a large baking sheet and coat both sides with 2 tablespoons olive oil and a generous sprinkling of salt and pepper. Toss potatoes with another 2 tablespoons olive oil and a generous sprinkling of salt and pepper. Place potatoes, cut side down, on a second large baking sheet. Toss asparagus with remaining 1 tablespoon olive oil and a generous sprinkling of salt and pepper.

Adjust oven racks to lowest and upper-middle positions. Place potatoes on bottom rack and salmon on upper rack of cold oven, then heat oven to 400 degrees. Roast until salmon is just opaque throughout, about 25 minutes, and potatoes are golden brown, about 30 minutes. Transfer salmon to a large platter. Add asparagus to salmon baking sheet and roast, along with potatoes, until bright green and just tender, 5 to 8 minutes, depending on thickness. Meanwhile, mix parsley, dill leaves, capers and juice, scallions, lemon zest and extra-virgin olive oil in a small bowl.

Arrange potatoes and asparagus on platter with salmon, garnishing with dill sprigs and lemon slices. Serve immediately, passing sauce separately.

DRINK **An Oregon Pinot Gris or West Coast Chardonnay**

APPETIZER Shrimp Wonton Crisps with Asian Pesto

Crisp wonton chips, herbaceous Asian pesto, sweet peanuts, briny shrimp—all the makings of a terrific nibble. The wonton crisps can be stored in a tin for several days, the pesto can be covered and refrigerated for a week or more, and the shrimp are bought precooked. When you're ready to serve this appetizer, it's just quick assembly.

1   medium garlic clove

3   tablespoons honey-roasted peanuts, plus 2 tablespoons chopped for garnish

¼   teaspoon crushed red pepper flakes

2   cups packed fresh cilantro leaves

3   tablespoons vegetable oil, plus 1 cup for frying

1   teaspoon sugar

1   teaspoon soy sauce

9   wonton wrappers, quartered

18   cooked peeled shrimp (31–35 count), halved lengthwise

Mince garlic, 3 tablespoons peanuts, and pepper flakes in a food processor. Add cilantro, 3 tablespoons oil, sugar, and soy sauce and process to pesto consistency.

Heat remaining 1 cup oil over medium heat in a medium skillet. When oil starts to shimmer, add 12 wonton quarters; fry, turning once, until golden brown, about a minute. Transfer to a wire rack. Repeat twice with remaining wontons.

Just before serving, place a shrimp half on each wonton crisp. Top with a generous ¼ teaspoon pesto, and garnish with a sprinkling of chopped peanuts.

INSTANT ALTERNATIVE: Serve Crispy Egg Roll Bites with Duck Sauce. Pick up 6 cooked egg rolls from your local Chinese restaurant (they are significantly better than store-bought frozen). Twenty minutes before serving, heat oven to 200 degrees and heat 2 cups vegetable oil over medium-high heat in a Dutch oven or small soup kettle until a small piece of bread sizzles when dropped in (350 to 375 degrees). Fry egg rolls, turning them once, until crisp and golden brown, about 2 minutes. Drain on a wire rack set over a baking sheet and place in warm oven until ready to serve. Quarter each roll on the diagonal, dipping one cut end in ¼ cup chopped fresh cilantro. Place cut side up on a serving tray and serve with ½ cup store-bought duck sauce mixed with 2 teaspoons rice wine vinegar. (Makes 2 dozen)

Deviled Eggs on Butter Lettuce with Honey-Mustard Dressing

SERVES 6

The honey-mustard mixture does double duty here, flavoring the deviled-egg stuffing and dressing the tender butter lettuce on which the eggs are served. To boil eggs, place the eggs in a medium saucepan, making sure they fit in a single layer. Cover with cold water, then the lid, and bring to a full boil over medium-high heat. Remove from heat, and let stand, covered, for 10 minutes. Drain and run cold water over the eggs in the saucepan until the pan has completely cooled. Add ice cubes to the water in the pan to cool the eggs as quickly as possible.

The dressing, filling, and eggs can be covered and refrigerated separately overnight.

½ **cup light mayonnaise**

3 **tablespoons Dijon mustard**

2 **tablespoons honey**

4 **teaspoons rice wine vinegar**

Salt and freshly ground black pepper

6 **boiled eggs (see headnote)**

2 **heads Boston lettuce, leaves separated**

Whisk mayonnaise, mustard, honey, vinegar, and salt and pepper to taste in a small bowl. Peel eggs and halve lengthwise; remove yolks and place in a small bowl. Mash 5 tablespoons dressing into yolks to make a smooth filling.

Just before serving, spoon (or pipe) a portion of yolk mixture into each egg white half. Gently toss lettuce with enough of the remaining dressing to lightly coat. Arrange a portion of lettuce leaves on each of six salad plates. Top each with 2 deviled eggs. Drizzle with a little additional dressing, if desired, and serve.

Meringue Pastries with Strawberry Sauce

SERVES 6

In this new, lightened take on strawberry shortcake, a puff-pastry crust stands in for the usual biscuit or cake, while sweetened egg whites replace the heavy cream. Both the strawberry sauce and the meringue-topped pastries can be made several hours ahead. Just cover the sauce and refrigerate, and let the pastries stand out at room temperature.

- **1 package (12 ounces) frozen strawberries, partially thawed (1–1½ minutes on high power in microwave)**
- **½ cup strawberry jelly**
- **2 cups fresh strawberries, hulled and sliced, plus 6 whole strawberries, halved lengthwise**
- **1 sheet frozen puff pastry (from a 17.3-ounce box), thawed**
- **1 tablespoon cornstarch**
- **6 large egg whites**
- **1 teaspoon vanilla extract**
- **¾ cup sugar**

Puree partially thawed berries and jelly in a blender until smooth, and stir in sliced berries. Refrigerate, covered, until ready to serve.

Adjust oven rack to lower-middle position and heat oven to 425 degrees. Unfold pastry onto a floured work surface and, following fold lines and rolling up and down, roll dough out to a 12-by-10-inch rectangle. Halve dough crosswise and cut into thirds along fold lines to make 6 rectangles. Place on a large baking sheet and prick several times with a fork. Place another baking sheet over pastry to prevent it from puffing. Bake, removing top sheet after 15 minutes, until crisp and golden brown, 18 to 20 minutes. Remove from oven and reduce oven temperature to 325 degrees.

Meanwhile, bring cornstarch and ⅓ cup water to a simmer in a small saucepan over medium-high heat, whisking constantly until mixture thickens and turns translucent. Beat egg whites and vanilla in a large bowl with an electric mixer until frothy. Gradually add sugar; beat to soft peaks. Add warm cornstarch mixture; beat to stiff peaks.

Mound a portion of the meringue over each pastry. Bake until golden brown, 15 to 20 minutes. Pastries can be served warm or at room temperature. Just before serving, spoon a portion of sauce onto each of six plates and set a pastry meringue in each pool of sauce. Garnish with 2 strawberry halves and serve.

INSTANT ALTERNATIVE: Assemble Strawberry Cream Parfaits with Coconut Macaroon Crumble. Toss 1 quart sliced strawberries (about 3 cups) with 6 tablespoons sugar; set aside. Beat 1½ cups heavy cream, ¾ teaspoon finely grated orange zest, and 1½ tablespoons sugar in a medium bowl with an electric mixer to soft peaks. Crumble 3 cups store-bought macaroons (about 8 ounces) into a medium bowl and pour accumulated strawberry juices over macaroons. Toss to coat. In each of six goblets, make 2 layers of the following: scant ¼ cup macaroons, scant ¼ cup whipped cream, and ¼ cup strawberries. Refrigerate for up to 2 hours before serving.

Balsamic-Glazed Chicken Breasts

WITH MUSHROOM–GOAT CHEESE STUFFING AND BRUSSELS SPROUT (OR GREEN PEA) RISOTTO

With its robust goat-cheese-flavored mushroom filling, this classy, complete roast-chicken dish works well for fall, winter, and early spring. Flavor the risotto with Brussels sprouts in the fall and winter months and with green peas for spring.

APPETIZER Roasted Mixed Nuts
Instant Alternative: Warm Roasted Almonds

SALAD Greens with Smoked Trout (or Salmon), Red Onion, and Capers

DESSERT Warm Bread Pudding with Chocolate and Brandied Cherries
Instant Alternative: Brandy-Spiked Brownie and Cherry Parfaits

Balsamic-Glazed Chicken Breasts
with Mushroom–Goat Cheese Stuffing
and Brussels Sprout (or Green Pea) Risotto

SERVES 8

If possible, try to find the smaller, more attractive 10- to 12-ounce bone-in, skin-on chicken breasts. If you can't, the 1-pound breasts work fine; just pound them with your fists to flatten them before stuffing. You may want to consider splitting this size between two guests.

Before stuffing the chicken breasts, take time to trim them a bit. They'll look more attractive with the protruding rib bones and excess skin cut away. For chicken breasts with skimpy skin, it's OK if some of the mushroom filling peeks out from under the skin. The chicken can be stuffed, glazed, covered with plastic wrap, and set aside for up to 2 hours or refrigerated overnight; return to room temperature before roasting. Also, the onion and rice can be sautéed and set aside for 2 hours or covered and refrigerated overnight.

1 ounce dried mushrooms (your choice of variety)

4 large garlic cloves

1 pound white or baby bella mushrooms, brushed if dirty, coarsely chopped

1 teaspoon dried thyme leaves

½ stick (4 tablespoons) butter, divided

6 ounces mild goat cheese

Salt and freshly ground black pepper

1 container (2 heaping cups) Brussels sprouts or 1 cup frozen peas (not thawed)

1 large onion, chopped

2 cups Arborio rice

¼ cup honey

¼ cup balsamic vinegar

8 split bone-in, skin-on chicken breasts, protruding rib bones and excess fat trimmed, rinsed, and patted dry (see headnote)

1 quart chicken broth

¾ cup finely grated Parmesan cheese

Microwave 2 cups water and dried mushrooms in a 1-quart Pyrex measuring cup on high power until boiling hot, about 4 minutes. Let stand until softened, about 5 minutes. Remove mushrooms from liquid. When cool enough to handle, squeeze mushrooms dry. Reserve liquid, straining if it appears gritty.

Mince garlic in a food processor fitted with the metal blade. Add rehydrated mushrooms and process to mince. Add fresh mushrooms and thyme and process until all ingredients are minced.

Heat 2 tablespoons butter in a large heavy roasting pan set over two burners on medium-high heat. Add mushroom mixture and cook, stirring, until nearly all the moisture has evaporated, about 5 minutes. Scrape mixture into a medium bowl, stir in goat cheese, and season to taste with salt and pepper; set aside. If using Brussels sprouts to flavor risotto, use slicing disk of food processor to shred them at this time or shred with a sharp knife; set aside.

Heat remaining 2 tablespoons butter in unwashed roasting pan over medium-high heat. Add onion and cook, stirring, until softened, 3 to 4 minutes. Add rice, stir to coat, and turn off heat. Mix honey and vinegar in a small bowl.

Being careful not to overcrowd, set chicken breasts, skin side down, on a wire rack in roasting pan. Brush with honey-vinegar mixture and season generously with salt and pepper. Turn chicken breasts over, making sure thick ends face outer edge of pan, where meat will cook faster. Carefully lift skin on one side of each chicken breast and stuff with a portion of goat cheese filling. Brush with remaining honey-vinegar mixture and season with salt and pepper.

About an hour before serving, adjust oven rack to lowest position and heat oven to 425 degrees. Stir broth and reserved mushroom liquid into rice in roasting pan. (If you prepared chicken breasts ahead, return them to a wire rack over roasting pan.) Roast until chicken is golden brown (a meat thermometer inserted into the thickest portion of the largest piece should register 160 degrees) and rice has absorbed broth, 35 to 40 minutes (time will vary depending on size of chicken breasts).

Transfer chicken to a platter. Stir Parmesan and shredded Brussels sprouts or green peas into risotto. Arrange a chicken breast on each of eight plates along with a portion of risotto and serve.

DRINK **A full-bodied dry white like Verdicchio or, for a red, a light Barbera**

APPETIZER Roasted Mixed Nuts

MAKES 2 HEAPING CUPS

These roasted nuts are rich and attractive, salty, spicy, sweet, and aromatic, with a hint of orange. If making these in the spring, you can use blanched almonds in place of the mixed nuts. You can also substitute an equal amount of fresh rosemary for the thyme. The nuts can be stored in an airtight container for up to 1 month.

1¼ pounds roasted salted premium mixed nuts

2 tablespoons minced fresh thyme leaves

1 teaspoon finely grated orange zest

2 teaspoons packed dark brown sugar

2 teaspoons paprika

½ teaspoon cayenne pepper

½ teaspoon kosher salt

1½ tablespoons butter

Adjust oven rack to middle position and heat oven to 350 degrees. Spread nuts on a 13-by-9-inch metal baking pan. Toast until fragrant and very hot, 10 to 12 minutes.

Meanwhile, mix thyme, zest, brown sugar, paprika, cayenne, and salt in a small bowl. Microwave butter in another small bowl until melted; stir thyme mixture into butter. Pour hot nuts into a large bowl. Add thyme mixture and stir until completely coated. Pour nuts back onto baking pan and cool. Serve warm or at room temperature.

> **INSTANT ALTERNATIVE:** Serve Warm Roasted Almonds. If available, Spanish Marcona almonds are especially appealing. Warm them in a 350-degree oven for 5 to 8 minutes to refresh the roasted flavor.

SALAD # Greens with Smoked Trout (or Salmon), Red Onion, and Capers

SERVES 8

If serving this salad in early spring, substitute an equal amount of thinly sliced smoked salmon, cut into thin strips, for the trout. Adding 1½ teaspoons finely grated lemon zest and/or 2 tablespoons chopped fresh dill to the salad provides even more flavor. You can toss the salad with ¾ cup Lemon-Shallot Vinaigrette (page 234) instead of the dressing here, if you like.

10	ounces (about 15 cups) prewashed mixed baby greens
8	ounces smoked trout, skinned and broken into bite-size chunks (see headnote)
½	medium red onion, thinly sliced
⅓	cup drained capers
6–8	tablespoons extra-virgin olive oil
	Salt and freshly ground black pepper
1½–2	tablespoons fresh lemon juice

Place greens, trout, onion, and capers in a large bowl. Just before serving, toss with 6 tablespoons olive oil and a generous sprinkling of salt and pepper. Taste, adding more oil, salt, or pepper, if necessary. Add 1½ tablespoons lemon juice; toss to coat, adding more, if necessary, to taste, and serve.

Warm Bread Pudding with Chocolate and Brandied Cherries

SERVES 8

Cubes of soft bread absorb and become one with the rich vanilla custard in this bread pudding, decadently punctuated with chunks of bittersweet chocolate and brandy-plumped dried cherries. The cooking technique ensures perfection. Baking these delicate custards in a water bath cushions them from the oven's harsh heat, resulting in an irresistibly silky texture. The custard-soaked bread can be covered and refrigerated overnight. Just return it to room temperature before baking or allow a little extra oven time.

- 1 **cup dried cherries**
- ¼ **cup brandy**
- 3 **cups half-and-half**
- ½ **cup sugar**
- 2 **large eggs plus 2 large yolks**
- 1 **teaspoon vanilla extract**
- 5 **cups ¾-inch bread cubes from soft white bread**
- 4 **ounces bittersweet chocolate, cut into small chunks (scant 1 cup)**

Mix cherries and brandy in a small bowl. Heat half-and-half and sugar in a medium saucepan until steamy hot. Meanwhile, whisk eggs and yolks in a medium bowl and gradually whisk in hot-milk mixture. Stir in vanilla, then bread. Let stand until mixture has cooled to room temperature, about 15 minutes or up to 2 hours.

Adjust oven rack to lower-middle position and heat oven to 350 degrees. Spray eight 6-ounce custard cups with vegetable-oil cooking spray. Bring 1 quart of water to a boil for a water bath.

Set custard cups in a roasting pan. Stir cherries and any unabsorbed brandy into custard and divide evenly among custard cups, making sure some cherries sit on top. Top each cup with chocolate chunks, pressing some into custard and sitting some on top. Set pan on oven rack. Pour in enough boiling water to come halfway up sides of cups. Bake until custards are just set, about 30 minutes. Remove from oven and let stand for 10 to 15 minutes before serving.

INSTANT ALTERNATIVE: Make Brandy-Spiked Brownie and Cherry Parfaits. Bring ¼ cup brandy and 1 cup dried cherries to a simmer in a small saucepan. Turn off heat, cover, and let stand until cherries soften, just a couple of minutes. Meanwhile, mix ¼ cup brandy with 1 teaspoon instant espresso powder until dissolved. Using a serrated knife, halve 8 store-bought brownie bites crosswise (found in the baking department or cookie aisle of the supermarket). Generously brush each cut half with espresso mixture.

In each of eight parfait glasses, assemble 2 layers of each of the following: ½ brownie bite (it's OK if it falls apart), a 3-tablespoon scoop premium chocolate or vanilla ice cream (you'll need a scant 3 cups total), and 1 tablespoon dried cherries. Parfaits can be assembled and frozen several hours ahead; let stand at room temperature for a couple of minutes before serving.

Festive Roast Chicken and Stuffing

In this dish, which is every bit as special as roast turkey, the herb-rubbed chicken and stuffing bake together. As a result, the stuffing tastes as though it's been cooked in the bird, but it's done in a fraction of the time. There's a mix of light and dark meat for everyone: no carving required. Full of fresh herbs, dried apricots, and celery, the stuffing is a complete side dish on its own, but if you're serving buffet-style, you may want to add a salad. For a sit-down dinner, you can serve the salad first and then add a simple green vegetable—beans, peas, or Brussels sprouts—to the plate with the chicken.

APPETIZER Baked Camembert with Cranberry-Orange Relish
Instant Alternative: Port-Spiked Stilton and Dried Cranberry Bites

SALAD Warm Broccoli, Cauliflower, and Red Bell Pepper Salad

DESSERT Pumpkin Custards with Ginger and Cinnamon
Instant Alternative: Pumpkin-Gingersnap Ice Cream

Festive Roast Chicken and Stuffing

SERVES 8

The chicken can be rubbed with the spice, the bread cubes toasted, and the sausage and vegetables cooked up to 2 days in advance. After that, you just brown the chicken, mix the stuffing, bake, and serve. If you need to bake this dish in a disposable pan, remember that the thin foil will not retain heat like a heavy roasting pan, so you'll need to increase the baking time by 10 to 15 minutes.

10–12 cups ½-inch bread cubes, plus 2 cups finely ground fresh bread crumbs (use a food processor) from a couple loaves of dense, crusty Italian or French bread

3 tablespoons Italian seasoning, divided

1 tablespoon plus ¾ teaspoon salt, divided

2½ teaspoons freshly ground black pepper, divided

2 teaspoons fennel seeds, minced

1½ teaspoons finely grated orange zest

2 tablespoons olive oil

8 bone-in, skin-on chicken thighs (about 4 pounds), trimmed, rinsed, and patted dry

4 large split bone-in, skin-on chicken breasts (about 4 pounds), protruding rib bones and excess fat trimmed, rinsed, patted dry, and halved crosswise

1 pound bulk Italian sausage or 1 pound links, casings removed

2 medium onions, chopped (about 2 cups)

3 medium celery stalks, chopped (about 1 cup)

1½ cups golden raisins or finely chopped dried Turkish apricots

½ cup minced fresh parsley

2 large eggs

1 quart chicken broth

Spread bread cubes in a single layer on a large baking sheet and spread bread crumbs on a separate baking sheet; let dry for several hours or overnight.

Adjust oven rack to lower-middle position; heat oven to 400 degrees. Bake bread cubes until golden brown, 12 to 15 minutes. (Do not toast crumbs.) Remove from oven and reduce oven temperature to 350 degrees.

Meanwhile, mix 2 tablespoons Italian seasoning, 1 tablespoon salt, 2 teaspoons pepper, fennel, orange zest, and oil in a small bowl. Smear mixture over both sides of each piece of chicken.

Heat a large heavy roasting pan over two burners on medium-high heat. When wisps of smoke start to rise from pan, add chicken in 2 batches (breasts skin side down). Cook until skin is well browned (3 to 4 minutes), turn, and cook until chicken breasts lose their raw color on remaining side and skin on thighs is well browned, another couple of minutes. Remove from pan and set aside.

Add sausage to roasting pan and fry, stirring frequently to break it up, until it loses its raw color, about 5 minutes. Add onions and celery to pan and continue to cook until vegetables are soft, 7 to 8 minutes. In a large bowl, mix bread cubes, bread crumbs, sausage mixture, raisins or apricots, parsley, remaining 1 tablespoon Italian seasoning, remaining ¾ teaspoon salt, and remaining ½ teaspoon pepper. Whisk eggs into broth in a medium bowl and pour over stuffing ingredients. Toss to coat and let stand for 10 minutes so bread absorbs broth.

Turn stuffing into unwashed roasting pan. Top with chicken, skin side up, and bake until attractively brown and chicken is fully cooked, about 45 minutes. Remove from oven and let stand for 10 minutes before serving.

DRINK An Alsatian white, a buttery West Coast Chardonnay, or, for red, a delicate, fruity Pinot Noir

APPETIZER Baked Camembert with Cranberry-Orange Relish

SERVES 8

Warm pastry-encased Camembert topped with sweet-tart cranberry sauce is the perfect start to a festive winter meal. The cranberry sauce can be covered and refrigerated for up to 2 weeks. The unbaked pastry-encased cheese can be covered and refrigerated overnight. If there's no time to let the Camembert rest to firm up, have a box of water crackers on hand so your guests can spread the cheese on the crackers.

1 **bag (12 ounces) fresh or frozen cranberries, rinsed and picked over**
1 **cup sugar**
   Finely grated zest and juice from 1 large orange
1 **sheet frozen puff pastry (from a 17.3-ounce box), thawed**
1 **wheel Camembert cheese (about 4 inches in diameter), top rind sliced off**

Bring cranberries, sugar, and orange juice to a full simmer in a medium skillet or a 5- to 6-quart Dutch oven. Simmer for 1 minute. Cover, turn off heat, and let stand for 10 minutes. Stir in orange zest, cool to room temperature, and refrigerate.

Adjust oven rack to lower-middle position and heat oven to 425 degrees. Roll puff pastry on a lightly floured surface along the fold lines to 12 inches long. Cut out two 6-inch rounds. Lay one pastry round on a baking sheet and set cheese wheel on it, cut side up. Top with remaining puff pastry round and crimp around perimeter of cheese to seal.

Bake until pastry is golden brown, about 20 minutes. Let rest for 15 minutes and serve, letting each person slice a wedge of the pastry-encased cheese and top with cranberry sauce.

INSTANT ALTERNATIVE: Make Port-Spiked Stilton and Dried Cranberry Bites. Bring 1 cup dried cranberries and ½ cup port to a full simmer in a small saucepan. Cover, turn off heat, and let stand until cranberries are plump and have absorbed port, about 5 minutes. Soften 1½ cups (about 8 ounces) dry crumbly Stilton cheese in a microwave for about 15 seconds. Mash cheese with ½ cup port in a medium bowl until well incorporated (it may seem wet at first, but cheese will eventually absorb it). Smear a generous teaspoon of blue cheese on each of 24 bite-size whole-wheat bagel crisps (a 6-ounce bag will do). Garnish with a few cranberry pieces. Both cheese and cranberries can be refrigerated separately in airtight containers for weeks. (Makes 2 dozen hors d'oeuvres)

Warm Broccoli, Cauliflower, and Red Bell Pepper Salad

SERVES 8 TO 10

The bell pepper and garlic can be cooked up to 2 hours ahead.

3   **tablespoons olive oil**

1   **large red bell pepper, stemmed, seeded, and cut into short, thin strips**

3   **large garlic cloves, minced**

6   **cups broccoli florets**

6   **cups cauliflower florets**

¼   **cup drained capers**

   Salt

   Lemon-Shallot Vinaigrette (page 234)

Heat oil in a large skillet over medium-high heat. Add pepper strips and cook, stirring, until golden, 3 to 4 minutes. Add garlic and continue to cook, stirring, until fragrant, about 30 seconds longer. Add broccoli, cauliflower, capers, and ⅔ cup water seasoned with 1 teaspoon salt. Increase heat to high, cover, and steam until vegetables are just tender and water has almost evaporated, about 5 minutes. Using tongs, divide vegetables among salad plates, drizzling each with a generous tablespoon vinaigrette, and serve.

Pumpkin Custards with Ginger and Cinnamon

SERVES 8

Although silky smooth in texture and rich in flavor, these pumpkin custards are light in calories, thanks to evaporated milk, making them the perfect end to a rich holiday meal. The custards can be made a couple of days in advance, provided you lay plastic wrap directly on the surface of each custard to prevent a skin from forming. If you've got a culinary torch, finish the custards brûlée-style, by sprinkling each with ½ teaspoon brown sugar and torching until it has a crisp sugar top.

- ½ **cup pure pumpkin (from a 15-ounce can)**
- ½ **teaspoon ground ginger**
- ½ **teaspoon ground cinnamon**
- ½ **cup packed dark brown sugar**
- 2 **cups evaporated milk**
- 1 **large egg plus 2 large yolks**

Bring 1 quart water to a boil for a water bath. Set eight 6-ounce custard cups in two 8-inch square pans (disposable pans work well). Adjust oven rack to lower-middle position and heat oven to 325 degrees.

Heat pumpkin, ginger, and cinnamon in a medium saucepan over medium heat until puree sputters and flavors intensify, 3 to 4 minutes. Whisk in brown sugar, then evaporated milk, and bring to a simmer. Meanwhile, whisk egg and yolks in a medium bowl. Gradually whisk hot-pumpkin mixture into eggs, then pour into custard cups. Set pans in oven and carefully pour in enough hot water to come halfway up sides of cups. Bake until custards are set, about 30 minutes. Remove custard cups from baking dish and cool slightly. Lay plastic wrap directly over each custard to prevent a skin from forming. Chill until ready to serve.

INSTANT ALTERNATIVE: Pumpkin-Gingersnap Ice Cream is one of my favorite cool-weather desserts. Heat 1 can (15 ounces) pure pumpkin, 1 teaspoon ground ginger, ½ teaspoon ground cinnamon, and ¼ teaspoon ground cloves in a medium saucepan over medium heat, stirring to blend flavors, about 5 minutes. Transfer to a shallow bowl and place in freezer to cool quickly. Meanwhile, soften 1 quart premium vanilla ice cream (15 to 30 seconds on high power in microwave). Turn into a large bowl and stir in cooled pumpkin puree until nearly incorporated. Crumble 16 crisp gingersnaps into ice cream and continue to fold until incorporated. Freeze to stiffen slightly, 10 to 15 minutes, until ready to serve. You can freeze any leftover ice cream, but if you want the cookies crisp, serve within a few hours.

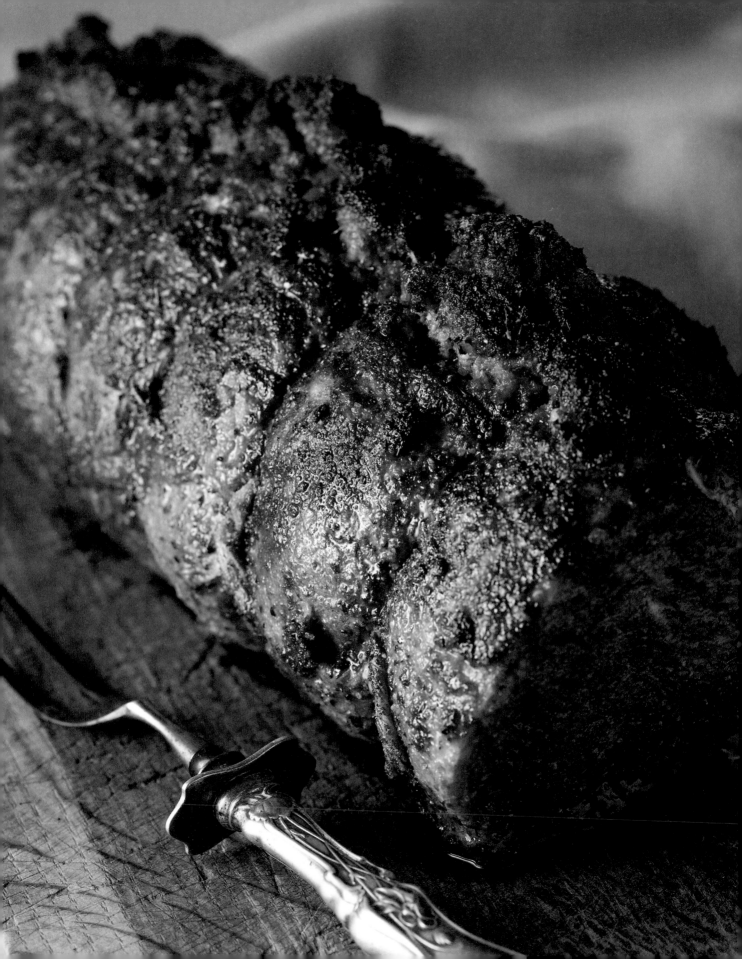

Roast Chorizo-Stuffed Adobo Pork Loin

WITH BLACK BEANS AND RICE

This is the ticket when you are expecting a houseful of guests. Since whole pork loins sell for under $2 a pound at big-box food stores like Costco, there just isn't a classier, cheaper way to feed a crowd. The black beans and rice, which cook under the pork during the last 20 minutes of cooking, are the beneficiaries of the roast's spicy pan drippings. Leftover pork can be turned into an amazing pot of chili—just use your favorite recipe, shred the pork into bite-size pieces, and substitute it for the beef.

APPETIZER Make-Ahead Jack Quesadillas with Salsa Verde
Instant Alternative: Jack Nachos with Salsa Verde

SALAD Greens with Apples, Dried Cherries, and Roasted Pumpkin Seeds

DESSERT Silky Chocolate Flan
Instant Alternative: Mocha Tartlets

Roast Chorizo-Stuffed Adobo Pork Loin

with Black Beans and Rice

SERVES 16 (OR 8, WITH ANOTHER MEAL OF LEFTOVERS)

If you don't want to cook such a large roast, buy a 3½- to 4-pound pork loin, halve the remaining ingredients, and roast it in a smaller pan to serve 8. Since a smaller roast is shorter—not thinner—the cooking time should not differ dramatically. The roast can be stuffed and seasoned, then refrigerated (no need to cover) up to a day ahead.

16	large garlic cloves, peeled
6	tablespoons olive oil, divided
1	pound fully cooked chorizo sausage, cut into large chunks
1	cup fresh whole cilantro leaves, plus 1 cup chopped
¼	cup chipotle chiles in adobo sauce (from a 7-ounce can)
¾	cup plain dry bread crumbs
3	tablespoons ground cumin, divided
2	tablespoons plus 2 teaspoons kosher salt, divided
1	tablespoon plus 1½ teaspoons freshly ground black pepper, divided
2	tablespoons ground paprika
2	tablespoons packed light or dark brown sugar
1	whole boneless pork loin (6–8 pounds; see headnote)
4	cans (15–16 ounces each) black beans, drained
1	quart chicken broth
2	cups long-grain rice
1	can (14.5 ounces) petite diced tomatoes, undrained
1	bunch scallions, thinly sliced (about 1 cup)

Heat garlic cloves and 3 tablespoons oil in a small skillet over medium heat. Once garlic starts to sizzle, reduce heat to low and continue to cook, turning cloves once or twice, until soft and golden, 5 to 7 minutes.

Meanwhile, place chorizo, 1 cup whole cilantro leaves, chipotles, bread crumbs, and 1 tablespoon cumin in a food processor bowl. Add garlic and its oil and process until ingredients are finely ground; set aside.

Mix remaining 2 tablespoons cumin with 2 tablespoons salt, 1 tablespoon pepper, paprika, and brown sugar in a small bowl.

Adjust oven rack to lower-middle position and heat oven to 250 degrees. Lay pork loin on a sheet of plastic wrap, fat side down. Slit pork loin lengthwise down center almost—but not quite—all the way through to form a long pocket. Brush cavity with 1 tablespoon oil and sprinkle with remaining 2 teaspoons salt and remaining 1½ teaspoons pepper.

Line cavity with sausage mixture. Tie roast crosswise with butcher's twine at 1½-inch intervals, alternating between one end and the other so stuffing remains even.

Brush roast with remaining 2 tablespoons oil and sprinkle all over with cumin-paprika mixture.

Place roast on a wire rack set in a large heavy roasting pan and roast until a meat thermometer inserted into center registers 125 to 130 degrees, about 1½ hours. Increase oven temperature to 400 degrees. Remove rack with pork from pan and add beans, broth, rice, and tomatoes. Stir and return rack with roast to pan and return pan to oven. Continue to roast until a meat thermometer inserted into center of pork registers 155 to 160 degrees, about 20 minutes longer. Transfer to a carving board and let rest, uncovered, for 15 to 20 minutes. Meanwhile, stir scallions and remaining 1 cup chopped cilantro into beans and rice; cover and keep warm. Just before serving, cut roast into ½-inch-thick slices. Place on individual dinner plates and spoon some rice and beans alongside.

DRINK   **A full-bodied Zinfandel**

APPETIZER Make-Ahead Jack Quesadillas with Salsa Verde

MAKES 4 DOZEN TRIANGLES

Many of us make quesadillas like grilled cheese—one at a time in a skillet. It's possible, however, to make them for a large group. Simply heat both sides of each flour tortilla in a dry skillet. (When the skillet gets hot, it takes only about 45 seconds per tortilla.) Assemble the quesadillas on a large baking sheet. They are already crisp, so you only need to bake them long enough to melt the cheese. Since you're already chopping cilantro and scallions for the rice and beans for the roast pork, you may want to chop a little extra of one or the other (or both) to sprinkle on the cheese before baking the quesadillas.

16 small (6-inch) flour tortillas

4 cups grated Monterey or pepper Jack cheese (about 12 ounces)

¼ cup chopped fresh cilantro

1 jar (16 ounces) store-bought salsa verde (2 cups)

Adjust oven racks to lower- and upper-middle positions and heat oven to 375 degrees. Heat a small skillet over medium-high heat. When wisps of smoke start to rise from pan, add 1 flour tortilla and cook until spotty brown, about 30 seconds on the first side and 15 seconds on the second side; repeat with remaining tortillas.

Arrange 4 tortillas on each of two baking sheets, sprinkle each with ½ cup cheese. Top each with one of the remaining tortillas. Bake until cheese melts, changing baking sheet positions and rotating the sheets back to front after 6 minutes, if necessary, for even cooking, about 10 minutes total. Stir cilantro into salsa verde. Cut each quesadilla into 6 triangles and serve with the salsa verde as a dipping sauce.

INSTANT ALTERNATIVE: Make Jack Nachos with Salsa Verde. To serve 16, you'll need a 16-ounce bag of tortilla chips, 4 cups grated Monterey Jack cheese, and ¾ cup thinly sliced scallions. Arrange one quarter of the chips in a more or less single layer on a large ovenproof platter. Sprinkle with 1 cup cheese and one quarter of the scallions and repeat, making 3 more layers. Bake in a 250-degree oven until chips are warm and cheese melts, 10 to 15 minutes (although it doesn't hurt to leave them in the oven longer to keep them warm). Serve with store-bought salsa verde.

SALAD Greens with Apples, Dried Cherries, and Roasted Pumpkin Seeds

SERVES 16 (HALVE RECIPE IF SERVING 8)

Whether served as a first course or on the same plate as the roast, this salad of crisp apples and sweet dried cherries calms the spicy chorizo-stuffed pork. The salad is also good tossed with about 1 cup Balsamic Vinaigrette (page 27) or Orange Vinaigrette (page 18).

20	ounces (about 30 cups) prewashed mixed baby greens
4	crisp, tart apples, cored and chopped
1	cup dried cherries
1	cup hulled roasted salted pumpkin seeds
¾–1	cup extra-virgin olive oil
	Salt and freshly ground black pepper
3–4	tablespoons balsamic or rice wine vinegar

Place greens, apples, dried cherries, and pumpkin seeds in a large bowl. Just before serving, toss with ¾ cup olive oil and a generous sprinkling of salt and pepper. Taste, adding more oil, salt, or pepper, if necessary. Add 3 tablespoons vinegar; toss to coat, adding more, if necessary, to taste, and serve.

DESSERT Silky Chocolate Flan

SERVES 8 (DOUBLE RECIPE IF SERVING 16)

Flan ranks among my favorite desserts. Adding chocolate moves it to the very top of the list. If making two flans, bake them back-to-back, adding the second flan to the water bath when the first one comes out. Or bake them simultaneously in a double oven.

1	cup sugar
1	can (12 ounces) evaporated milk
4	ounces unsweetened chocolate
½	teaspoon instant coffee powder
4	large eggs
1	teaspoon vanilla extract
1	can (14 ounces) sweetened condensed milk

Adjust oven rack to center position and heat oven to 325 degrees. Bring 1 quart water to a boil for a water bath. Set a 9-inch deep-dish pie plate in a roasting pan or a large, deep skillet big enough to accommodate it.

Whisking constantly, bring sugar and ¼ cup water to a boil over medium heat in a medium heavy-bottomed saucepan. When mixture starts to boil, turn heat to medium-low and stop whisking. Continue to simmer until mixture turns golden brown, about 10 minutes. Pour mixture into pie plate. Immediately pour evaporated milk into saucepan and return to heat. Add chocolate and coffee powder and whisk until chocolate just melts. Remove from heat.

Meanwhile, whisk eggs, one at a time, along with vanilla, into condensed milk in a large bowl. Immediately whisk chocolate mixture into egg mixture in a steady stream.

Set roasting pan in oven and pour flan batter into pie plate. Pour hot water into roasting pan until it comes halfway up sides of pie plate. Bake until flan is jiggly, but set, about 30 minutes. Remove from oven, cool to room temperature, and refrigerate. Just before serving, run a small knife around pie plate perimeter to loosen flan. Invert onto a large lipped platter, cut into wedges, and serve.

INSTANT ALTERNATIVE: Serve Mocha Tartlets (double recipe to serve 16). Whip 1 cup heavy cream, 2 tablespoons sugar, 2 teaspoons instant espresso powder, and 1 teaspoon vanilla extract in a medium bowl with an electric mixer to stiff peaks. Place 1 Famous Chocolate Wafer (you'll need a total of 32 cookies) in each of eight foil muffin cups (papers removed). Top each with 1 tablespoon whipped cream. Repeat 3 more times, gently pressing cookie into whipped cream. Sprinkle the final dollop of whipped cream with a little shaved or grated bittersweet or semisweet chocolate. Refrigerate until cookies soften, 3 to 4 hours. Serve.

Blue Cheese–Stuffed Beef Tenderloin

WITH PORT SAUCE AND MUSHROOM-SPINACH BARLEY

Holiday roasts are simple. It's coordinating all the side dishes that can be stressful. Here, beef tenderloin stuffed with blue cheese roasts over mushroom-flavored barley, with fresh baby spinach stirred in at the last minute. It's festive, and you need nothing more.

APPETIZER Crisp Potato Bites with Smoked Salmon, Sour Cream, and Chives

SALAD Greens with Pomegranate, Grapefruit, and Red Onion

DESSERT Vanilla-Raspberry Trifle
Instant Alternative: Nanny's Victoria Sponge

Blue Cheese–Stuffed Beef Tenderloin
with Port Sauce and Mushroom-Spinach Barley

SERVES 8, WITH LEFTOVERS

Unless you have an extra-large crowd or very big eaters, you'll likely have leftover beef and barley. If so, make a pot of soup. Cook a large finely chopped onion in a little olive oil in a soup pot. Add leftover beef, shredded into small bites, blue cheese stuffing, barley, and chicken broth to cover; bring to a boil. Reduce heat to low and simmer, partially covered and adding more broth, if necessary, until flavors blend, 20 to 30 minutes. The soup can be refrigerated for up to 5 days and freezes well too.

1   **trimmed beef tenderloin (about 4 pounds)**

    Salt and freshly ground black pepper

¾   **teaspoon dried thyme leaves, divided**

2½ **cups crumbled blue cheese (10–12 ounces), divided**

⅓   **cup plain dry bread crumbs**

3   **tablespoons olive oil, divided**

1   **cup port wine**

1   **cup plus 2 quarts chicken broth, divided**

1   **large onion, chopped**

1   **pound (about 2½ cups) pearl barley**

1   **heaping cup dried mushrooms (about 1 ounce), cut into bite-size pieces if large**

1   **cup dry white wine**

7   **ounces (about 10 cups) prewashed baby spinach**

1   **cup coarsely grated Parmesan cheese**

1   **teaspoon cornstarch dissolved in 1 teaspoon water**

Slit tenderloin lengthwise almost, but not quite, all the way through, to form a long pocket. Sprinkle tenderloin with ¼ teaspoon salt, ½ teaspoon pepper, and ½ teaspoon thyme. Mix 2 cups blue cheese, bread crumbs, ¼ teaspoon pepper, and remaining ¼ teaspoon thyme in a small bowl. Stuff beef with blue cheese mixture. Tie tenderloin crosswise at 1½-inch intervals with butcher's twine, alternating between one end and the other so that roast is evenly stuffed. Coat with 1 tablespoon oil and sprinkle generously with salt and pepper.

Adjust oven rack to lower-middle position and heat oven to 425 degrees. Heat a large heavy roasting pan over two burners on medium-high heat. When wisps of smoke begin rising from the pan, turn on exhaust fan and sear roast until well browned, about 2 minutes on each of its four sides; transfer to a baking sheet. Reduce heat under roasting pan to low and add port, scraping pan to loosen brown bits. Pour port into a medium saucepan, along with 1 cup chicken broth. Reduce to 1 cup; whisk in remaining ½ cup cheese; set aside.

Meanwhile, add remaining 2 tablespoons oil to pan. Add onion and cook, stirring, until tender and well browned, 4 to 5 minutes. Add barley and cook, stirring constantly, until lightly toasted, 1 to 2 minutes. Stir in dried mushrooms, then white wine, and simmer until nearly evaporated. Add remaining 2 quarts chicken broth and bring to a simmer. Set a wire rack in the roasting pan and set roast on rack. Set pan in oven and cook until a meat thermometer inserted into thickest portion of roast registers 120 degrees for medium-rare or 125 degrees for medium, 30 to 35 minutes. Remove roast from rack and rack from pan. Let roast rest uncovered, return barley to oven, and continue to cook until liquid evaporates and barley is tender with a little chewiness, about 20 minutes longer. Remove from oven and stir in spinach and Parmesan, stirring until spinach wilts. Return port sauce to a simmer and whisk in cornstarch mixture to thicken slightly. Transfer warm barley to a serving bowl. Cut tenderloin into 1-inch-thick slices and serve with port sauce.

DRINK **A brut sparkling wine to start, followed by a rich red, such as Cabernet or Merlot**

APPETIZER Crisp Potato Bites with Smoked Salmon, Sour Cream, and Chives

MAKES 2 DOZEN HORS D'OEUVRES

For a simple, sumptuous hors d'oeuvre, just bake frozen hash browns until crispy and top with thinly sliced smoked salmon, a dollop of sour cream, and a pinch of fresh chives.

- **6 frozen hash brown patties**
- **6 ounces thinly sliced smoked salmon**
- **¼ cup sour cream**
- **2 tablespoons finely snipped fresh chives**

Adjust oven rack to lowest position and heat oven to 450 degrees.

Place patties on a nonstick baking sheet (or one that's been coated with vegetable-oil cooking spray). Bake until patties start to crisp, about 7 minutes. Turn them and continue to bake until crisp and golden brown, 7 to 8 minutes longer.

Transfer hash browns to a cutting board, topping each with an ounce of smoked salmon. Quarter each patty and dollop each portion with ½ teaspoon sour cream and a sprinkling of chives. Serve.

SALAD Greens with Pomegranate, Grapefruit, and Red Onion

SERVES 8

This rich meal begs for a crisp, clean salad. You can toss the salad with ¾ cup Orange Vinaigrette (page 18) instead of the oil and vinegar here, if you prefer.

2	large grapefruits
10	ounces (about 15 cups) prewashed mixed baby greens
1	heaping cup pomegranate seeds
½	medium red onion, thinly sliced
6–8	tablespoons extra-virgin olive oil
	Salt and freshly ground black pepper
1½–2	tablespoons balsamic or rice wine vinegar

With a large knife, cut off tops and bottoms of grapefruits and stand on end. Slicing along sides, cut off rind and pith using a small sharp knife. Working over a bowl to catch juice, slice between membranes to cut out segments. Cut into large chunks.

Place greens, grapefruit and juice, pomegranate seeds, and onion in a large bowl. Just before serving, toss with 6 tablespoons olive oil and a generous sprinkling of salt and pepper. Taste, adding more oil, salt, or pepper, if necessary. Add 1½ tablespoons vinegar (and a little of the grapefruit juice, if you like) and toss to coat, adding more, if necessary, to taste, and serve.

DESSERT Vanilla-Raspberry Trifle

SERVES UP TO 12

Here's a grand finale to a celebration dinner. To partially thaw the berries, simply microwave them on high power for 1 to 1½ minutes. Both the pudding and the raspberry puree can be covered and refrigerated for up to 3 days before assembly. The trifle is best made a day ahead.

1	**quart whole milk**
1¼	**cups sugar, divided**
¼	**cup cornstarch**
¼	**teaspoon salt**
4	**large egg yolks**
2	**tablespoons vanilla extract, divided**
1	**package (12 ounces) frozen raspberries, partially thawed (see headnote)**
½	**cup seedless raspberry jam**
2	**cups heavy cream**
3	**tablespoons brandy or cognac**
2	**containers (about 6 ounces each) fresh raspberries, 12 reserved for garnish**
16	**ounces pound cake, sliced ½ inch thick**
⅔	**cup cream sherry**

Microwave milk in a 2-quart Pyrex measuring cup or in a small bowl until steamy hot, 4 to 5 minutes. Meanwhile, whisk 1 cup sugar, cornstarch, and salt in a large saucepan. Whisk in yolks, set over medium heat, and vigorously whisk in hot milk. Continue to whisk until mixture thickens to pudding consistency, about 4 minutes. Remove from heat and stir in 4 teaspoons vanilla. Transfer pudding to a medium bowl, cover surface directly with a sheet of plastic wrap to prevent a skin from forming, and cool to room temperature.

Meanwhile, puree partially thawed berries and jam in a food processor. Push through a fine-mesh sieve to strain out seeds and refrigerate.

Just before assembly, whip cream and remaining ¼ cup sugar in a medium bowl with an electric mixer to stiff peaks. Slowly beat in brandy or cognac and remaining 2 teaspoons vanilla extract.

Assemble trifle in a 4-quart glass bowl in the following order: 1 cup pudding, one quarter fresh raspberries, one quarter cake slices generously brushed with sherry, ¾ cup whipped cream, ½ cup raspberry puree. Repeat 3 more times. Top trifle with remaining whipped cream and garnish with reserved raspberries. Cover and refrigerate until ready to serve.

INSTANT ALTERNATIVE Nanny's Victoria Sponge

SERVES 8

Although not technically "instant," this simple from-scratch cake—the recipe courtesy of my son-in-law's grandmother—is utter perfection.

If you want to substitute all-purpose flour for the self-rising flour, whisk 1½ teaspoons baking powder and ¼ teaspoon salt into the flour.

1½ **sticks (12 tablespoons) unsalted butter, softened**

1 **cup sugar**

3 **large eggs**

1½ **cups self-rising flour (see headnote)**

1 **teaspoon vanilla extract**

½ **cup seedless raspberry jam**

Confectioners' sugar for sprinkling

Adjust oven rack to lower-middle position and heat oven to 350 degrees. Grease and flour two 8-inch round cake pans.

Beat butter and sugar in a large bowl with an electric mixer until light and fluffy. Alternately add eggs and flour in thirds, beating until each is thoroughly incorporated before adding the next third. Beat in 1 tablespoon warm water and vanilla. Divide batter between prepared pans.

Bake until golden brown, about 20 minutes. Remove from oven, let stand for a couple of minutes, then turn out onto a wire rack to cool to room temperature. Spread top of one cake with jam and top with remaining cake. Dust with confectioners' sugar, slice, and serve.

Big Summer Salads and Grilled Platters

Lemony Seafood Pasta Salad

WITH TOMATOES, FETA, AND OREGANO

Light on pasta, heavy on seafood, and bold in flavor, this salad is stunning enough for a dressy summer party, yet homey enough for a casual potluck. Adding bay scallops and shrimp to the cooking pasta not only contributes briny flavor but also keeps this main-course salad utterly simple.

APPETIZER Deviled Eggs with Green Olives, Thyme, and Smoked Paprika
Instant Alternative: Quick Egg Salad with Green Olives, Thyme, and Smoked Paprika

DESSERT Ouzo-Flavored Blood Orange Sorbet
Instant Alternative: Fruit Sorbet in a Pool of Ouzo

Lemony Seafood Pasta Salad
with Tomatoes, Feta, and Oregano

SERVES 8

For color contrast, roasted yellow peppers are preferable. If they're not available, use roasted reds. The salad can be prepared a day ahead, but for peak freshness, toss it with the dressing close to serving. Leftovers are great for a day or two—just pop them in the microwave for a few seconds to take off the chill.

1 large garlic clove, minced

3 tablespoons fresh lemon juice

2 tablespoons Dijon mustard

1 tablespoon rice wine vinegar

Salt and freshly ground black pepper

½ cup extra-virgin olive oil

½ pound bite-size pasta, such as penne

1 pound bay scallops

1 pound (31–35 count) uncooked shrimp, preferably wild, peeled, deveined, halved lengthwise, and cut into bite-size pieces

1 cup grape tomatoes, halved and lightly salted

½ cup diced jarred roasted yellow peppers (see headnote)

4 ounces crumbled feta cheese (about ¾ cup)

¼ cup chopped fresh oregano

Whisk garlic, lemon juice, mustard, vinegar, and a light sprinkling of salt and pepper in a Pyrex measuring cup. Slowly whisk in olive oil to make a thick dressing; set aside.

Meanwhile, bring 2 quarts water and 1 tablespoon salt to a boil in a large pot. Add pasta and, using package times as a guide, cook until just tender, about 10 minutes. Add seafood to pasta and continue to cook until seafood is just opaque, a minute or so longer. Drain (do not run under cold water) and pour onto a baking sheet to cool. Just before serving, mix pasta and seafood, tomatoes, roasted peppers, cheese, and oregano in a large bowl. Add dressing, toss to coat, and serve.

DRINK   A clean, crisp white, such as **Vernaccia di San Gimignano or Sancerre**

APPETIZER # Deviled Eggs with Green Olives, Thyme, and Smoked Paprika

MAKES 16

Smoked paprika is relatively common on the spice rack of many grocery stores and offers a distinct smokiness to the eggs. If unavailable, substitute regular paprika or simply omit. The filled eggs can be covered and refrigerated for several hours.

  8 large boiled eggs, peeled (see headnote on page 180)
  3 tablespoons coarsely chopped pimento-stuffed salad olives
  1½ tablespoons drained capers
  ½ teaspoon dried thyme leaves
  3 tablespoons olive oil
     Smoked paprika for sprinkling (see headnote)

Halve eggs crosswise and remove yolks. Trim rounded bottom of each white slightly to stabilize egg.

Process egg yolks in a food processor until very fine. Add olives, capers, and thyme and pulse until olives are finely chopped, about 4 short bursts. Add olive oil and pulse once or twice until just incorporated. Fill each egg half with a portion of the olive mixture. Sprinkle with smoked paprika and serve.

> **INSTANT ALTERNATIVE:** Make Quick Egg Salad with Green Olives, Thyme, and Smoked Paprika. Mix 6 large boiled eggs, chopped, with ½ cup coarsely chopped salad olives, 3 tablespoons mayonnaise, 1½ teaspoons Dijon mustard, 1 teaspoon minced fresh thyme leaves, and a sprinkling of salt and pepper. Mound on a plate. Sprinkle generously with smoked paprika and serve with your favorite flatbread crackers or bagel or pita crisps. (Makes 2 cups, serving 8)

Ouzo-Flavored Blood Orange Sorbet

SERVES 8

This simple sorbet starts with good-quality, store-bought orange juice. Mix in sugar, liqueur, and lemon juice, and churn in your ice cream machine. That's it. The anise flavoring is light, but if you're not a fan, substitute 2 tablespoons vodka to keep the sorbet from freezing solid. You can also make the sorbet with other interesting juices—pomegranate or blueberry, for example, which are usually found, along with the blood orange juice, in the refrigerated section of the produce department—or use regular orange juice.

1 **quart chilled bottled or cartoned blood orange juice (see headnote)**

1 **cup sugar**

¼ **cup ouzo or other anise-flavored liqueur, such as Pernod, pastis, or sambuca (see headnote)**

2 **tablespoons fresh lemon juice**

Mix orange juice, sugar, ouzo, and lemon juice in a 1-quart Pyrex measuring cup until sugar completely dissolves. Following manufacturer's instructions, churn sorbet, in batches if necessary, in an ice cream machine until frozen. Store in freezer until ready to serve.

INSTANT ALTERNATIVE: Serve Fruit Sorbet in a Pool of Ouzo. Mix 3 tablespoons licorice-flavored liqueur, such as ouzo, sambuca, Pernod, or pastis, with 6 tablespoons water. Pour about 1 tablespoon of diluted liqueur into each of eight goblets. Spoon a portion of orange, mixed berry, or raspberry sorbet (you'll need 2 pints total) into each goblet and serve immediately.

Lobster Platter

Some of my best food memories are of sharing lobsters and all the fixings around a carefree summer table. One of the most impressive one-dish meals you can offer your guests, this platter is also one of the simplest—especially when you use a roasting pan rather than a pot.

APPETIZER Boston-Meets-Manhattan Clam Chowder
Instant Alternative: Steamed Clams with Tomatoes and Oregano

DESSERT Blueberry Cheesecake Ice Cream
Instant Alternative: Quick Berry Cobbler

Lobster Platter

SERVES 6

Setting a large heavy roasting pan over two burners is an especially efficient technique for cooking lobster with all the trimmings. The increased surface area allows you to steam 6 lobsters, complete with potatoes and corn, at one time—no bringing gallons of water to a boil! Because hard-shell lobsters are packed with meat (and are less watery), I prefer them to soft-shells. But soft-shell lobsters can be a good buy—especially during the summer months. If you opt for soft-shells, you may want to step up to the 1½-pound size. Placing the lobsters in the freezer for a few minutes before cooking makes them less frisky going into the pan. Leave them in the freezer too long, however, and their appendages may snap off.

2	pounds small red new potatoes
6	lobsters (about 1¼ pounds each), preferably hard-shell (see headnote)
6	ears corn, shucked
1½	sticks (12 tablespoons) butter, melted until hot
	Lemon wedges

Bring about 1 inch water and potatoes to a boil over high heat in a very large heavy (18-by-14-inch) roasting pan set over two burners. Cover with heavy-duty foil; cook for 5 minutes. Add lobsters to pan, placing them crosswise in 3 rows of 2 lobsters each, tails tucked under and lobsters facing each other. Cover with foil and cook for another 10 minutes. Lay corn in the nooks and crannies between lobsters (there will be a bit of a mound), re-cover, and cook until potatoes are tender, lobsters are pink and fully cooked, and corn is done, about 10 minutes longer. Turn off heat and let rest for a few minutes. Serve immediately with warm butter (2 tablespoons in each of six ramekins) and lemon wedges.

DRINK   **A Chardonnay from the West Coast or a French White Burgundy**

Boston-Meets-Manhattan Clam Chowder

SERVES 6, WITH LEFTOVERS

Rich, creamy Boston clam chowder could use a little zing. Brothy, red Manhattan clam chowder could stand a little cream. Choose the best from each—bacon and cream from Boston, tomatoes and a little heat from New York—and you've got a wonderfully appealing hybrid. Because of the bountiful meal ahead, you'll want only a small cup, but leftovers are great for tomorrow's lunch.

2	slices thick-cut bacon, cut into ½-inch pieces
1	large Spanish onion, chopped
1	teaspoon Italian seasoning
½	teaspoon crushed red pepper flakes
½	teaspoon garlic powder
¼	cup all-purpose flour
4	cans (6.5 ounces each) minced clams, clams and juice separated
2	bottles (8 ounces each) clam juice
1	can (14.5 ounces) petite diced tomatoes, drained
1½	pounds red boiling potatoes (about 9 new potatoes), cut into medium dice
1	cup heavy cream
2	tablespoons minced fresh parsley leaves
	Salt and freshly ground black or white pepper

Fry bacon in a large soup kettle over medium heat until fat renders and bacon crisps, about 5 minutes. Add onion to bacon and drippings and cook, stirring, until softened, about 5 minutes. Whisk in Italian seasoning, pepper flakes, and garlic powder, then whisk in flour, whisking until lightly colored, about 1 minute. Gradually whisk in juice from canned clams, bottled clam juice, tomatoes, and 1 cup water. Add potatoes and simmer until potatoes are tender, about 10 minutes. Add clams, cream, parsley, and salt and pepper to taste; bring to a simmer. Remove from heat and serve.

INSTANT ALTERNATIVE: Make Steamed Clams with Tomatoes and Oregano (use the same roasting pan you'll steam the lobsters in and cook the lobsters while your guests are enjoying the clams). Place 3 tablespoons olive oil, 4 minced garlic cloves, and 1 teaspoon dried oregano in a large heavy roasting pan set over two burners over medium-high heat. When garlic starts to sizzle, add 1 can (14.5 ounces) petite diced tomatoes, drained. Cook to intensify flavors and evaporate some of the juice, 1 to 2 minutes. Add ½ cup dry vermouth and 3 dozen (3 pounds) littleneck clams, rinsed thoroughly in cold water. Cover with heavy-duty foil and steam until clams open, 5 to 7 minutes, depending on size. Transfer clams and sauce to a large wide bowl, discarding any clams that do not open. Serve with a separate bowl alongside for shells. You can make this dish up to the point of adding the clams a few hours ahead. It's better to steam the clams just minutes before you're ready to sit down and enjoy them. You'll likely not have leftovers, but if you do, they're perfect for tossing with pasta (save the juice too).

Blueberry Cheesecake Ice Cream

SERVES 6 TO 8

End on a high note with graham cracker–studded ice cream, blueberry sauce, and a cream cheese topping. You can make the graham crackers (wrap them in foil or place them in an airtight tin), as well as the blue-berry sauce and sweetened cream cheese components (store separately in covered containers), a day or so before serving. So that the graham crackers stay crisp, however, it's best to hold off crumbling the crackers into the ice cream until a couple of hours before serving. Even though the crackers may not be as crisp the next day, leftover dessert is still pretty irresistible.

- **3 tablespoons butter**
- **½ cup sugar, divided**
- **6 whole graham crackers**
- **1 pint (2 cups) fresh or frozen blueberries**
- **2 teaspoons cornstarch mixed with 2 teaspoons cold water**
- **½ teaspoon finely grated lemon zest**
- **1 quart premium vanilla ice cream**
- **4 ounces cream cheese, softened**

Adjust oven rack to middle position and heat oven to 375 degrees. Line a baking sheet with parchment paper or a Silpat baking mat.

Heat butter and 2 tablespoons sugar in a medium saucepan until butter has melted. Arrange crackers close together on baking sheet. Brush butter mixture over crackers. Bake until golden brown and fragrant, about 7 minutes. Cool to room temperature. Quarter 2 of the crackers along perforated lines to make 8 sticks for garnish.

Meanwhile, bring blueberries and ¼ cup sugar to a full boil in same saucepan, 2 to 3 minutes. Stir in 1 teaspoon cornstarch mixture and cook until just thickened, almost immediately. If blueberries are especially juicy (or frozen), you may need to add remaining cornstarch mixture. Stir in lemon zest. Set aside.

Microwave ice cream on high power until softened slightly, about 15 seconds; turn into a medium bowl. Coarsely crumble remaining 4 whole graham crackers, then fold into ice cream. Return ice cream to freezer until ready to serve.

Meanwhile, whisk remaining 2 tablespoons sugar into cream cheese.

Just before serving, scoop a portion of ice cream into each dessert dish. Top with 2 tablespoons blueberry sauce and 1 tablespoon cream cheese mixture. Garnish with a graham cracker stick and serve immediately.

INSTANT ALTERNATIVE: Make Quick Berry Cobbler. Adjust oven rack to lower-middle position and heat oven to 375 degrees. Mix ½ cup sugar, 4 teaspoons cornstarch, 1 teaspoon finely grated lemon zest, and ¼ teaspoon salt in a small bowl. Place 2 quarts (about 8 cups) blueberries in a 13 by 9-inch pan, add sugar mixture, and toss to coat. Pinch half a 16.5-ounce log of sugar cookie dough into 16 pieces and place evenly over fruit. Bake until berries are bubbly and topping is golden brown, about 40 minutes. Let cool slightly, spoon into shallow bowls, top with premium vanilla ice cream, and serve.

Grilled Salad Niçoise

Big platters of grilled food and vegetables like this Niçoise salad are relatively simple to pull off, yet so appealing. Classic Niçoise accompaniments—new potatoes, plum tomatoes, and green beans—round out the meal, along with boiled-egg quarters and piquant olives. You can serve this platter hot, warm, or at room temperature.

APPETIZER Fresh Tomato-Basil Bread Soup
Instant Alternative: Fresh Tomato-Basil Yogurt Soup

DESSERT Lemon-Cooler Cookies and White Wine–Marinated Strawberries

Grilled Salad Niçoise

SERVES 8

The lemony vinaigrette doubles as both a marinade for the fish and a dressing for the platter. Depending on your preference, this dish can be served hot off the grill, warm, or even at room temperature. Leftovers are great for the next few days.

LEMON-SHALLOT VINAIGRETTE

- 2 medium shallots or 1 large, minced
- ¼ cup fresh lemon juice
- ¼ cup Dijon mustard
- 2 tablespoons rice wine vinegar
- ¼ teaspoon salt
- ¼ teaspoon freshly ground black pepper
- 1 cup extra-virgin olive oil

SALAD NIÇOISE

- 2¼–2½ pounds fresh tuna steaks, cut into 8 pieces
- 16 small red new potatoes (2¼ pounds), halved
- 8 plum tomatoes, halved lengthwise
- 1¼–1½ pounds green beans, trimmed
- 3 tablespoons extra-virgin olive oil
- Salt and freshly ground black pepper
- 8 large boiled eggs, peeled and quartered (to boil, see headnote on page 180)
- 32 black olives (niçoise or kalamata)

Lemon-Shallot Vinaigrette: Whisk shallots, lemon juice, mustard, vinegar, ¼ teaspoon salt, and ¼ teaspoon pepper in a small bowl or 2-cup liquid measuring cup. Slowly whisk in oil, first in droplets then in a steady stream, to make a thick vinaigrette.

Salad Niçoise: Coat tuna with ½ cup vinaigrette; set remaining vinaigrette aside.

Keeping potatoes, tomatoes, and green beans separate, toss each with 1 tablespoon oil and sprinkle generously with salt and pepper. Place green beans on a large wire rack. Heat gas grill, igniting all burners on high for at least 10 minutes, or build a hot charcoal fire. Clean grate with a wire brush, then use tongs to wipe a vegetable oil–soaked rag over grill rack.

Place potatoes and tomatoes on hot grill rack. Cover and cook, turning potatoes once and not turning tomatoes at all, until potatoes are grill-marked and cooked through and tomatoes are soft, about 10 minutes. Divide potatoes and tomatoes between two platters; set aside.

Close grill lid and return to hottest state. Place tuna on hot grill rack and place rack with green beans perpendicular to grill rack. Cover and cook, turning tuna once, until it is grill-marked on both sides and cooked to medium, 5 to 6 minutes, and turning green beans occasionally, until they are crisp-tender, about 10 minutes. Divide tuna and green beans and arrange on platters with potatoes and tomatoes. Arrange eggs over potatoes, tomatoes, green beans, and tuna, and scatter olives over each platter. Drizzle with remaining vinaigrette and serve.

DRINK **A Provençal or other dry rosé**

APPETIZER Fresh Tomato-Basil Bread Soup

SERVES 8

When made with ripe seasonal tomatoes and fragrant fresh basil, this soup is summer in a bowl. Adding fresh bread crumbs is a traditional Mediterranean technique for thickening and imparting marvelous body. Serve as an hors d'oeuvre in attractive cocktail glasses or small mugs or as a light first course at the table. The soup can be made earlier in the day and refrigerated; allow to come to room temperature before serving.

1½   cups lightly packed fresh basil leaves, plus 8 sprigs for garnish

3   large garlic cloves

3   pounds vine-ripened tomatoes (if large, cut into chunks)

12   ounces French baguette (about three-quarters of a loaf), crust removed and reserved for another use, crumb pulled into bite-size chunks

1   tablespoon kosher salt

2   tablespoons sherry vinegar

6   tablespoons extra-virgin olive oil

Working in 2 batches, mince half of basil leaves and garlic in a blender. Add half of tomatoes and 1½ cups ice-cold water and process until pureed. Repeat with remaining basil, garlic, and tomatoes and 1½ cups ice water. Strain through a fine-mesh sieve to remove solids. Return puree to blender in 2 batches, along with bread, salt, and vinegar. Process until very smooth, 30 seconds to a minute. Add olive oil; process to combine. Serve, garnishing with basil sprigs.

INSTANT ALTERNATIVE: Shave a little off prep time with Fresh Tomato-Basil Yogurt Soup. Mix 1 quart plain low-fat yogurt, 2 cans (14.5 ounces each) undrained petite diced tomatoes, 2 large sliced scallions, 1 cup fresh basil leaves, ¼ cup extra-virgin olive oil, 2 tablespoons rice wine vinegar, and salt and freshly ground black pepper to taste. Working in 2 batches, puree in a blender until smooth. Refrigerate until ready to serve.

DESSERT # Lemon-Cooler Cookies

MAKES ABOUT 2 DOZEN

Round off this meal with sugared strawberries spiked with white wine (recipe follows) and the simplest-ever lemon cookies. These cookies can be stored in an airtight tin for up to a week.

- 1 **cup bleached all-purpose flour**
- ¾ **cup confectioners' sugar, divided**
- 1 **teaspoon finely grated lemon zest**
- 1 **stick (8 tablespoons) unsalted butter, softened enough to be pliable**
- ¼ **teaspoon vanilla extract**

Adjust oven rack to lower-middle position and heat oven to 350 degrees. Line a baking sheet with parchment paper or a Silpat baking mat.

Mix flour, ¼ cup confectioners' sugar, and lemon zest in a medium bowl. Add butter and vanilla and beat or simply mix with your hands to form a smooth dough.

Roll generous teaspoons of dough into balls and place on baking sheet 1 inch apart. Bake until cookie bottoms are golden brown, about 15 minutes. Transfer cookies to a wire rack to cool completely.

Place remaining ½ cup confectioners' sugar in a quart-size zipper-lock bag. Working with a dozen cookies at a time, drop cookies into sugar; shake to coat. Serve.

DESSERT # White Wine–Marinated Strawberries

SERVES 8

- 2 **pounds strawberries, hulled, or 8 peaches, peeled and sliced**
- ¾ **cup sugar**
- 1½ **cups fruity white wine, such as Riesling**

Mix strawberries or peaches with sugar and wine in a medium bowl until sugar dissolves. Let stand for 30 minutes or up to 3 hours and serve.

> **INSTANT ALTERNATIVE:** To save time, you can pick up store-bought shortbread or other good-quality butter cookies instead of the Lemon-Cooler Cookies.

Grilled Antipasto Platter

The ingredients of a traditional antipasto platter—shrimp, sausage, summer vegetables, and olives—are transformed into a generous main course. Everything is grilled in batches: the eggplant and peppers first, followed by the zucchini, sausages, and tomatoes, and, finally, the shrimp and bread, if desired. Feta vinaigrette boldly unifies them all.

APPETIZER Miniature Crab Cakes with Basil and Scallions
Instant Alternative: Tortellini with Pesto-Ricotta Dip

DESSERT Plum-Almond Tart
Instant Alternative: Fresh Plums with Mascarpone and Honey-Roasted Almonds

Grilled Antipasto Platter

SERVES 8

If you don't have time to make the vinaigrette, simply drizzle the platter with a little extra-virgin olive oil and the juice of 1 fresh lemon, along with 1 teaspoon dried oregano and ½ cup crumbled feta cheese. For impressive grill marks, sprinkle the skewered shrimp with ¼ teaspoon sugar just before grilling.

If you'd like to serve grilled garlic bread with the platter, mince 4 large peeled garlic cloves in a food processor or blender. With the motor running, add 4 tablespoons extra-virgin olive oil and ½ stick (4 tablespoons) softened butter through the feeder tube and continue to process for 30 seconds; season with salt and freshly ground black pepper. Cut a 1-pound loaf of rustic Italian bread into ¾-inch slices and brush both sides with the garlic oil; sprinkle lightly with salt. Grill when instructed in the recipe. Like any grilled platter, this one can be served hot, warm, or at room temperature.

2	pounds hot or sweet Italian sausage links
2	pounds (12–15 count) unpeeled shrimp, preferably wild, threaded onto skewers
½	cup olive oil, divided
3	baby eggplants, untrimmed, sliced lengthwise into quarters
3	medium zucchini, untrimmed, sliced lengthwise into quarters
3	yellow bell peppers, untrimmed, sliced lengthwise into quarters
8	large plum tomatoes, halved lengthwise
	Salt and freshly ground black pepper
½	cup piquant black olives, such as kalamata
	Feta Vinaigrette (optional, but very good; see headnote; recipe follows), divided
¼	cup crumbled feta cheese

Bring sausages and ⅔ cup water to a boil in a covered large (12-inch) skillet over high heat. Continue to cook until sausages lose their raw color and water evaporates, about 5 minutes.

Brush skewered shrimp with 2 tablespoons olive oil.

Toss eggplants, zucchini, peppers, and tomatoes with remaining 6 tablespoons olive oil and season with salt and pepper. (If grilling bread, prepare now; see headnote.)

Meanwhile, heat a gas grill, with all burners on high, for at least 10 minutes. Or, 45 minutes to an hour before serving, build a hot charcoal fire. Clean grate with a wire brush, then use tongs to wipe a vegetable oil–soaked rag over grill rack. Close lid and return to temperature.

Place eggplants and peppers on hot grate; cover and grill, turning only once, until impressive grill marks form on both sides, about 10 minutes. Arrange on a large platter and set aside.

Closing lid and returning grill to temperature between batches, repeat grilling with zucchini, sausages, and tomatoes, cut side up, turning zucchini and sausages only once and not turning tomatoes at all, until zucchini and sausages are grill-marked and tomatoes are soft, about 10 minutes. Add to platter.

Repeat grilling with shrimp (and bread, if using), turning only once, until grill-marked on both sides, 4 to 5 minutes. Remove shrimp from skewers and add to platter, along with olives.

Drizzle the antipasti with ½ cup Feta Vinaigrette, if using, and sprinkle with feta cheese. Serve, passing remaining vinaigrette.

Feta Vinaigrette

MAKES ABOUT 1 CUP

The vinaigrette can be made several hours ahead, and leftovers store well in the refrigerator for up to a week. Bring to room temperature before serving.

  2 **tablespoons Dijon mustard**

  2 **tablespoons red wine vinegar**

  1 **tablespoon rice wine vinegar**

  2 **large garlic cloves, minced**

  1 **teaspoon dried oregano**

  ¼ **teaspoon salt**

  ¼ **teaspoon freshly ground black pepper**

  ½ **cup extra-virgin olive oil**

  ½ **cup crumbled feta cheese**

Whisk mustard, vinegars, garlic, oregano, salt, and pepper in a small bowl or 2-cup liquid measuring cup. Slowly whisk in oil, first in droplets, then in a steady stream, to make a thick vinaigrette. Whisk in feta.

DRINK **A mellow but full-bodied red, such as Nero d'Avola or Barbera**

Miniature Crab Cakes with Basil and Scallions

MAKES 2 DOZEN

I like my crab cakes simple. The more flavor you add, the more you mask the crab's pure sweet taste. Serve these lightly flavored crab cakes with a bowl of tiny lemon wedges. Or mix up Lemon Dipping Sauce by stirring together ½ cup mayonnaise, ½ teaspoon finely grated lemon zest, and 1 tablespoon fresh lemon juice.

The formed cakes can be covered and refrigerated a day ahead. The cooked cakes can be transferred to a wire rack and kept warm in the oven for up to 30 minutes.

- 1 large egg, beaten
- 2 tablespoons mayonnaise
- 3 medium scallions, thinly sliced (about ¼ cup)
- ¼ cup chopped fresh basil
- ½ teaspoon hot red pepper sauce
- 1 pound jumbo lump crabmeat, drained
- 4 teaspoons milk
- 10 saltine crackers, crushed (about ½ cup)
- 6 tablespoons olive oil

Mix egg, mayonnaise, scallions, basil, and pepper sauce in a small bowl. Mix crabmeat and milk in a medium bowl. Add saltines to crabmeat and toss gently to combine. Add egg mixture and toss gently to combine. Press 2 tablespoons crab mixture into a compact cake. Repeat with remaining mixture to make 24 cakes.

Just before serving, heat oil in a large (12-inch) skillet over medium heat. Carefully add crab cakes to skillet. Cook, turning once, until golden brown, about 3 minutes per side. If not serving right away, transfer to a wire rack and keep warm in a 200-degree oven. Arrange on a platter. Serve with lemon wedges or Lemon Dipping Sauce, if desired (see headnote).

> **INSTANT ALTERNATIVE:** For a simpler nibble, pick up some quick-cooking cheese tortellini for Tortellini with Pesto-Ricotta Dip. Following package instructions, boil a 9-ounce package of fresh three-cheese tortellini (found in the refrigerated section of the supermarket) in 2 quarts water seasoned with 1 tablespoon salt; drain and toss with a little extra-virgin olive oil. Meanwhile, mix ½ cup ricotta cheese with ⅔ cup store-bought or homemade pesto in a small bowl. Use picks to dip warm tortellini into pesto-ricotta dip.

DESSERT Plum-Almond Tart

SERVES 8

You can make variations on this simple tart year-round, using figs in the fall and apples or pears in fall and winter. Switch to strawberries in spring. Summer offers several other options: blueberries, blackberries, peaches, or apricots. Top the tart, if you like, with a small dollop of mascarpone cheese.

1 **sheet frozen puff pastry (from a 17.3-ounce box), thawed**

2 **tablespoons sugar, divided**

5 **large plums, halved, pitted, and cut into eighths (see headnote)**

1 **scant cup grated almond paste (about 5 ounces;
   available in the supermarket baking aisle or gourmet section)**

Adjust oven rack to lowest position and heat oven to 425 degrees. Roll pastry out on a lightly floured surface to a 16-by-11-inch rectangle. Transfer to a 15-by-10-inch jelly-roll pan; do not stretch. Sprinkle pastry with 1 tablespoon sugar. Making sure they don't overlap, arrange plums lengthwise in 4 rows. Sprinkle with grated almond paste, then remaining 1 tablespoon sugar. Bake until golden brown, about 20 minutes. Slide onto a cutting board, cut into pieces, and serve.

> **INSTANT ALTERNATIVE:** Fresh Plums with Mascarpone and Honey-Roasted Almonds. Halve and pit 8 ripe plums. Set 2 halves in each dessert bowl, one resting on an angle against the other. Top each plum half with a heaping teaspoon mascarpone cheese (from an 8-ounce container). Drizzle with 2 teaspoons honey and sprinkle with 1 tablespoon honey-roasted sliced almonds.

Tandoori Platter

Boneless chicken is quick to cook, but it can dry out on a searingly hot grill. Not here. Marinating the thighs and breasts in yogurt and Indian seasonings keeps them deliciously moist. This impressive platter full of summer vegetables—eggplants, bell peppers, and zucchini, seductively seasoned with the same spice blend you use for the chicken—can be served hot, warm, or at room temperature.

APPETIZER Indian Six-Layer Dip
Instant Alternative: Classic Hummus

SALAD Raita

DESSERT Light, Lush Strawberry Milkshakes

Tandoori Platter

Serve this mouthwatering platter with a little grilled garlic naan, if you like. Here's how: For every two 9-inch naan breads (from an 8-ounce package), mix 4 minced garlic cloves, 2 tablespoons softened butter, and 2 tablespoons extra-virgin olive oil; brush over one side of each bread. Once chicken and vegetables are grilled, reduce heat to low, and place naan, buttered side up, on grill rack. Grill bread, turning once, until golden brown on both sides, about 3 minutes total.

My daughter loves the pot of soup I make from the leftovers. For Tandoori Chicken Soup, cut the leftover tandoori chicken and vegetables into bite-size pieces. If you don't have any leftover grilled onion, chop a large onion and cook, stirring, in 1 tablespoon olive oil in a large pot over medium-high heat until softened, about 5 minutes. Add 1 can (13.5 or 14 ounces) light coconut milk, ½ to 1 can (14.5 ounces) undrained petite diced tomatoes, 2 cans (about 16 ounces each) drained chickpeas, leftover tandoori chicken and vegetables, and chicken broth to cover. Simmer, partially covered, to blend flavors, about 15 minutes. Stir in a little chopped fresh cilantro and a little cayenne pepper for extra spice.

- ¼ **cup ground cumin**
- 1½ **tablespoons curry powder**
- 2 **teaspoons garlic powder**
- 1½ **teaspoons ground ginger**
- 1 **tablespoon salt**
- ¾ **teaspoon cayenne pepper**
- ½ **cup olive oil**
- 3 **small eggplants, sliced lengthwise into quarters**
- 3 **medium zucchini, halved crosswise, then lengthwise**
- 2 **medium bell peppers, preferably red, yellow, or orange, quartered lengthwise**
- 4 **small onions, halved across the equator (no need to peel)**
- 6 **tablespoons red wine vinegar**
- 1 **cup plain low-fat yogurt**
- 6 **medium boneless, skinless chicken breasts (about 2½ pounds)**
- 9 **medium boneless, skinless chicken thighs (about 2 pounds)**

Mix cumin, curry powder, garlic powder, ginger, salt, and cayenne in a medium bowl. Mix a generous ¼ cup spice mixture with oil, drizzle over vegetables in a large bowl, and toss to coat. Stir remaining spice mixture, along with vinegar, into yogurt; toss with chicken in another large bowl.

Up to 2 hours before serving, heat gas grill, with all burners on high, for 10 to 15 minutes, or build a hot charcoal fire. Use a wire brush to clean grill rack, then use tongs to wipe a vegetable oil–soaked rag over grill rack. Close lid and return to temperature. Have water close by to extinguish any flare-ups.

Place chicken on hot grill rack, cover, and cook until impressive grill marks form, about 5 minutes. Turn chicken over, cover, and continue to grill until remaining side is grill-marked and chicken is cooked through, about 5 minutes longer. Remove chicken from grill. Return grill to high heat and add vegetables; cover and grill until impressive grill marks form, about 5 minutes. Turn vegetables over; continue to grill until remaining side is grill-marked and vegetables are crisp-tender, about 5 minutes longer.

Halve chicken breasts, and arrange chicken and vegetables on a large platter. Serve hot, warm, or at room temperature with grilled garlic naan, if you like (see headnote).

DRINK **A Gewürztraminer or an Indian beer, such as Taj Mahal or Kingfisher**

APPETIZER Indian Six-Layer Dip

SERVES UP TO 12

Although not especially authentic, there's no mistaking the meal with which this rather intriguing, slightly addictive dip should partner. If you make this dip once, I can almost guarantee that it will become part of your regular repertoire. The dip can be made up to several hours ahead, covered, and refrigerated.

1	**cup light or regular sour cream**
1	**tablespoon curry powder**
1	**cup grated sharp cheddar cheese**
1	**cup Greek-style yogurt**
½	**cup Major Grey Chutney**
½	**cup sweetened flaked coconut**
½	**cup sliced scallions**
½	**cup roasted salted peanuts**
1	**bag pita chips, rice crackers, or pappadams**

Mix sour cream and curry powder and spread in a small shallow pie plate or gratin pan. Sprinkle with cheese. Mix yogurt and chutney and spread over cheese. Sprinkle with coconut and scallions. Just before serving, sprinkle with peanuts. Serve with chips, crackers, or pappadams.

INSTANT ALTERNATIVE: Freshen up a store-bought 8-ounce container of classic hummus by stirring in about 1 teaspoon fresh lemon juice, 1 teaspoon ground cumin, and salt to taste. Mound in a soup bowl, drizzle lightly with extra-virgin olive oil, and serve with a 6- to 8-ounce bag of store-bought baked pita chips.

MAKES ABOUT 3 CUPS

Serve this cooling Indian condiment with the spicy platter of chicken and vegetables. The raita can be made up to a day ahead and refrigerated, covered.

1 **large English cucumber, partially peeled (leave on some skin for color), halved, coarsely grated, and squeezed dry**

2 **cups plain low-fat yogurt**

¼ **cup chopped fresh mint**

1 **teaspoon ground cumin**

¼ **teaspoon cayenne pepper**

Salt

Mix grated cucumber, yogurt, mint, cumin, cayenne, and a generous pinch of salt in a medium bowl. Cover and refrigerate until just before serving.

Light, Lush Strawberry Milkshakes

SERVES 8

A refreshing end to the meal, this milkshake is almost instant. For Banana Milkshakes, substitute 8 medium-large frozen bananas for the strawberries and 2 teaspoons vanilla extract for the lemon juice.

2 containers (24 ounces each) frozen sweetened strawberries

2 cans (12 ounces each) 2% evaporated milk

2 teaspoons fresh lemon juice

8 fresh strawberries, cut lengthwise from the midpoint of bottom to within ¼ inch of top

Working in 2 batches, if necessary, place frozen strawberries, evaporated milk, and lemon juice in a blender and process until creamy smooth. Pour into eight small glasses, garnishing rim of each with a strawberry, and serve.

Grilled Steak and Potato Platter
WITH CHIMICHURRI SAUCE

Spice-rubbed steak, grilled potatoes, and summer-sweet corn come alive with a flavorful Argentinean-style chimichurri sauce. Olives and boiled eggs round out the platter.

APPETIZER Black and White Bean Caviar
Instant Alternative: Spicy Black Bean Dip

DESSERT Quick Tres Leches Cake

Grilled Steak and Potato Platter
with Chimichurri Sauce

SERVES 6 TO 8

You can buy more expensive steak—rib-eyes, strip steaks, filets mignons—for this attractive summer platter, but if you're serving a crowd, you might consider a cheaper—and more flavorful—cut, like beef loin flap meat steak, a robust cut from the belly. Because flap meat steak can be thin, cooking it to medium-rare or medium is ideal, as it will toughen otherwise. Boneless top sirloin steak and skirt steak are other reasonably priced options. When serving, slice across the grain.

If you like, garnish the steak and potatoes with pickled pink onions, made by mixing 1 halved, thinly sliced large red onion with 3 tablespoons rice wine vinegar and a sprinkling of salt and freshly ground black pepper. Let stand for 5 to 10 minutes or up to 2 hours.

Serve leftovers as a cold salad for lunch or dinner in the next day or two.

4	large garlic cloves, peeled
2	cups fresh parsley leaves
1	cup fresh cilantro leaves
1	jalapeño, stemmed and seeded
¾	cup extra-virgin olive oil
2	tablespoons fresh lemon juice
2	tablespoons rice wine vinegar
4	teaspoons dried oregano, divided
4	teaspoons ground cumin, divided
	Salt
2½–3	pounds beef loin flap meat steak, boneless top sirloin, or skirt steak (see headnote)
5	tablespoons olive oil, divided
	Freshly ground black pepper
2	pounds small red new potatoes, halved
6–8	ears corn, shucked and halved crosswise
6	large boiled eggs, halved lengthwise (see headnote on page 180)
1	cup kalamata olives
	Pickled onions (see headnote; optional)

Mince garlic, parsley, cilantro, and jalapeño in a food processor. Add extra-virgin olive oil, lemon juice, vinegar, 2 teaspoons oregano, 2 teaspoons cumin, and 1 teaspoon salt and continue to process until pureed. Transfer chimichurri sauce to a Pyrex measuring cup.

Rub steak with 2 tablespoons olive oil, remaining 2 teaspoons oregano, remaining 2 teaspoons cumin, and a generous sprinkling of salt and pepper.

Toss potatoes with 2 tablespoons olive oil and a generous sprinkling of salt and pepper. Toss corn with remaining 1 tablespoon olive oil.

About 30 minutes before serving, heat gas grill, with all burners on high, for 10 to 15 minutes, or build a hot charcoal fire. Use a wire brush to clean grill rack, then use tongs to wipe a vegetable oil–soaked rag over grill rack. Close lid and return to temperature. Have water close by to extinguish any flare-ups.

Place potatoes, cut side down, on hot rack, cover, and grill, turning, if necessary, after 5 minutes, until cooked through and impressive grill marks form on cut surface, about 10 minutes. Transfer potatoes to a medium bowl; add ½ cup chimichurri sauce and toss to coat.

Place steak and corn on hot rack, cover, and grill until steak is seared and corn is spotty brown on one side, about 5 minutes. Turn and continue to grill until steak is seared and corn is spotty brown on other side, 3 to 5 minutes longer, depending on steak's thickness and desired doneness. Arrange steak, potatoes, corn, eggs, and olives on a large platter. Top steak and potatoes with pickled onions, if you like, and pass remaining chimichurri sauce.

DRINK **A Malbec from Argentina**

APPETIZER Black and White Bean Caviar

SERVES 8 TO 12

The black and white mix of beans, the briny olives, and the slightly sweet stewed tomatoes and balsamic vinegar make this dip colorful and tasty. Although the white beans only need to be drained, be sure you rinse the black beans, or they will muddy the mixture. A batch of this keeps for weeks, covered, in the refrigerator. Use leftovers as a quick weeknight hors d'oeuvre or as a salad flavoring or dressing.

1 can (16 ounces) black beans, drained and rinsed
1 can (16 ounces) white beans, drained
1 can (14.5 ounces) stewed tomatoes, drained
1 cup drained pimento-stuffed green olives (from a 5-ounce jar)
2 medium jalapeños, stemmed, seeded, and minced
1 small onion, finely chopped
½ yellow bell pepper, chopped
¼ cup chopped fresh cilantro
¼ cup balsamic vinegar
6 tablespoons olive oil
½ teaspoon salt
½ teaspoon freshly ground black pepper
½ teaspoon garlic powder
1 teaspoon dried oregano
1½ teaspoons ground cumin
   Taste-Like-Fried Tortillas (page 154) or one 14- to 16-ounce bag store-bought tortilla chips

Mix all ingredients except tortilla chips in a medium bowl and let stand for a few minutes to allow flavors to develop. Just before serving, adjust seasonings, including vinegar, salt, and pepper. Serve with tortilla chips.

INSTANT ALTERNATIVE: Served with tortilla chips, Spicy Black Bean Dip is quick and yummy. Pulse ¼ cup packed cilantro leaves in a food processor until coarsely chopped. Add 2 cans (about 16 ounces each) drained black beans, along with 1 cup store-bought salsa and 1 teaspoon ground cumin. Pulse until coarsely chopped (do not process to a paste). Stir in ¼ minced small red onion and salt to taste. (For a spicier dip, stir in 1 teaspoon hot red pepper sauce.)

SERVES 8

This traditional Latin American "three-milks cake" is all about the milks—the cake is just the sponge. The shortcake's well becomes the perfect holding area as the cake absorbs the milk. You can serve the cake with flashier fruit, but the banana is a nice match for the milks' caramel hints. The cakes can be filled with milk, covered, and refrigerated overnight.

8   **shortcake dessert shells**

1   **can (14 ounces) sweetened condensed milk**

1   **can (12 ounces) evaporated milk**

½   **teaspoon vanilla extract**

1   **cup heavy cream**

2   **bananas, peeled and thinly sliced on the diagonal**

Place dessert shells on a baking sheet. Mix condensed milk, evaporated milk, and vanilla extract. Pour milk mixture into the well of each cake shell, refilling as cake absorbs it. (You will probably have between ⅓ and ½ cup milk mixture left over.)

Just before serving, whip cream to soft peaks in a medium bowl with an electric mixer. Fill each cake well with ¼ cup whipped cream, garnish with banana slices, and serve.

Index

Note: *Italicized* page references indicate photographs.